beauty care for the eyes

Books by LeRoy Koopman . . .
Beauty Care for the Eyes
Beauty Care for the Tongue

beauty care for the eyes

Leroy Koopman

ZONDERVAN PUBLISHING HOUSE

OF THE ZONDERVAN CORPORATION
GRAND RAPIDS, MICHIGAN 49506

BEAUTY CARE FOR THE EYES

Copyright © 1975 by The Zondervan Corporation
Grand Rapids, Michigan

Fourth printing   1978
ISBN 0-310-26832-X

Library of Congress Cataloging in Publication Data

Koopman, Leroy.
  Beauty care for the eyes.

  1. Spiritual life.   I. Title.
BV4501.2.K63   248'.4   75-21124

CONTENTS

PREFACE

This little volume is a companion piece to *Beauty Care for the Tongue*, published by Zondervan in 1974.

Both books are designed for group study as well as for private reading. A section, "Suggestions for Group Leaders," follows the body of the book.

The New Testament Scripture quotations are from the New International Version of the Bible. The Old Testament quotations are from the Revised Standard Version.

Dictionary definitions are from *The American Heritage Dictionary,* published by the American Heritage Publishing Co. and the Houghton Mifflin Company (1973).

I wish to express my gratitude to my loved ones and friends who by their encouragement and assistance made this little volume possible.

beauty care
for
the eyes

Chapter 1

Divine Ophthalmology

Let's get one thing straight right away.

The title of this book is misleading.

You might think, from the title, that this book is designed to help you have eyes that look beautiful.

It has nothing to do with that.

Not that the author has anything against beautiful eyes.

It's just that he feels it's more important to *see beautifully* than to *look beautiful*.

How you look out at the world is more basic to your happiness than how the world looks in at you.

Eyes are not just something to be looked at. They are something to look through.

It is far more important to see well than to look good.

Outlook is more important than inlook.

Outlook. That's what this book is all about.

Eyesight: A Cherished Possession

We have five senses — touch, smell, taste, hearing, and sight.

If you were told you would have to give up one of these, which would you pick?

Your answers may vary, but there is one capability I think none of us would choose to lose — the ability to see.

Sight is the most cherished of human sensibilities.

Through the eye-gate the whole world comes into our inner beings — loved ones, mountains, books, bugs, tele-

9

vision, roads, streams, stars, and all the other things, both beautiful and ugly, which enrich our existence.

Our eyes are among the most magnificent triumphs of God's creative power.

They can see a tiny gnat four inches away, then shift focus instantly to see a star billions of miles away.

They give us the privilege of living in a world of brilliant color.

By seeing three-dimensionally they enable us to determine such things as distance and velocity without using scientific instruments.

They can adjust from brilliant sunlight to a darkened room, and back again, within a few minutes.

They can move silently, swiftly, and effortlessly to follow any moving object we wish to watch.

Realizing the importance of our eyes, we spend much effort and money to protect and enhance them. We purchase eyeglasses or contact lenses. We wear sunglasses. We equip automobiles with safety glass. We shield them with our hands from flying sand. We put eye drops into them when they become inflamed. We secure the best medical treatment available for such eye ailments as sties, trachoma, glaucoma, and cataracts.

Since our eyes play such a vital role in our lives, it is not surprising that God, in His Word, often uses the symbol of eyesight to teach spiritual truths. He uses the imagery of physical perception to teach about spiritual perception.

The psalmist says, "Open my eyes, that I may behold wondrous things out of thy law" (Psalm 119:18).

God counsels the church at Laodicea to buy "salve to put on your eyes, so you can see" (Revelation 3:18).

Said Jesus, in the Sermon on the Mount, "The eye is the lamp of the body. If your eyes are good, your whole body will be full of light. But if your eyes are bad, your whole body will be full of darkness. If then the light within you is darkness, how great is that darkness!" (Matthew 6:22).

Not Used Just for Seeing

Eyes are not used only for seeing, of course.

They are flickered in seduction; they roll in exasperation; they stare vacantly in shock; they become narrow in anger; they wink in humor; they twinkle in fun; they flicker in recognition; they dart in fear; they sparkle in love; and they close in sleep.

The award for the most unusual use of the eyes goes to Rear Adm. Jeremiah A. Denton. In fact, he received just that — the Navy's second highest medal, the Navy Cross — for blinking his eyes. While being held a prisoner of war by the North Vietnamese in 1966, he was first tortured, then forced to submit to a propaganda interview with a Japanese newsman. While doing so he blinked out a Morse code distress message at the television camera, a message that was understood by U.S. naval intelligence officers.

Seeing Is Not Always Believing

It was James Thurber, I believe, who said, "Seeing is deceiving."

The women of Burma have for centuries walked behind their husbands, modestly and respectfully. Then immediately after World War II, a radical change took place. The Burmese beauties began to walk in front of their menfolk. The men not only permitted it graciously — they insisted upon it! "Ah, see the marvelous influence of American culture," we say. "Observe how we Westerners have taught those chauvinistic males to respect their wives."

But the full truth must be made known. It seems that after the war there were these unexploded land mines scattered all over the place . . .

Thurber was right. Seeing can be deceiving.

That's one reason why this book is being written. Our eyes can deceive us. They play tricks on us. Our facilities for perception can lead us to the wrong conclusions.

11

Things are not always the way they seem.

It is our hope that with the help of this little volume, each reader may improve his eyesight. Not simply in seeing, of course, but in *interpreting correctly* what he sees.

We See With Our Minds as Well as With Our Eyes

If we misinterpreted the scene of the Burmese men and women, the fault did not lie in the eye. The fault was in the mind. It took the photographic data correctly enough; but not having all the facts, it came to the wrong conclusion.

The mind is as responsible for seeing as the eye is. The eye cannot see without the mind. The impulses gathered by the eye are sent by means of the optic nerve to the brain, where they are sorted out and interpreted.

The image, when projected by the lens on the retina of the eye, is upside down. The brain places it right side up again.

If you were to see a picture of a ship with a giant, 250-foot man sitting on the prow, your mind would reject the notion of a giant and tell you that an ordinary man is sitting on a ship model.

If you were to view a picture of a camel with a head on each end, your brain would say, "It's a picture of two camels passing each other."

We see things, not necessarily as they are, but as they are interpreted for us by the brain.

That's why four people can stand on a street corner, witness an accident from the same vantage point, and give four different versions of what happened.

We Reveal Ourselves by What We See

I may show you a handful of change — halves, quarters, dimes, nickels, and pennies. What do you see? A child may see a dozen candy bars. A wife may see a bouquet of flowers. A husband may see a bill marked "paid." A coin collector may see dates and mint marks.

A cerebral palsy patient is struggling to walk down the street, his arms grotesquely bent, his head lolling sideways, his whole body veering crazily with each step.

One bystander may feel a lump in his throat as he looks with compassion and sympathy for he sees a poor, unfortunate creature.

A second bystander scowls because he sees a sickening, nauseating sight, a subhuman creature who ought to know enough to stay off the street and out of the view of sensitive people like himself.

A third person snickers. He sees a comical clown, and he thinks it's immensely funny. If there weren't others around, he might go over and trip that silly creature just for the fun of seeing him sprawling helplessly on the ground.

Yet a fourth person smiles in quiet approval. He sees, not an unfortunate or a comical creature, but an extraordinarily courageous human being who is managing to walk despite tremendous odds.

Here we have four pairs of eyes, each pair not physically different from the other three. The neurological and chemical processes are the same. There are no major biological defects. Yet each sees something quite different from the others.

What each person sees reveals a great deal about himself.

I once saw a fascinating film called *The Eye of the Beholder*. It pictured a few hours in the life of one Michael Gerard, bachelor. He has a short conversation with his mother, leaves in a hurry, hails a cab, meets his girl friend in a restaurant, and takes her to her apartment where they get into an argument. They scuffle and she falls to the floor.

This basic story is shown on the screen twice — once as seen through the eyes of the various people who had contact with Michael Gerard that day, and once as seen through the eyes of Gerard himself.

13

Gerard's mother sees him as a thoughtless and ungrateful son; the waiter in the restaurant sees him as a playboy; the cab driver sees him as a hoodlum; the janitor sees him as a lunatic; and the cleaning woman sees him as a lustful beast.

When the story is shown again, the basic facts, characters, and situations are the same. But there are subtle changes. Some of the sentences are stated differently. Some of the words have a different inflection. Facial expressions take on another significance. Scenes take on a new perspective. When seen through his mother's eyes, for instance, Michael's sudden departure is thoughtless and disrespectful. Through his own eyes, it is merely a matter of being in a hurry.

At the conclusion, the viewer doesn't really know exactly what was said or what interpretation to place on the incidents. But he has become convinced of two things: (1) what one sees depends as much on the eye of the beholder as it does on the objective fact; and (2) one tends to judge another's character by his own.

The Basic Problem

What is really important, then, in our perception of things? Is it not the condition of our minds and our hearts as well as that of our eyes?

The health of our seeing apparatus hinges on the health of our souls.

The accuracy of our eyes depends upon the truthfulness of our minds.

The perceptiveness of our eyes depends upon the spiritual perceptiveness of our souls.

But we know that something disastrous has happened to our hearts, minds, and souls — and hence to our eyes.

That disastrous thing is sin.

What took place in the Garden of Eden is a remarkable example. Before sin entered, the man and the woman were nude before each other without embarrassment or shame. But after sinning, they looked on each other differently, and they ran to find fig leaves. Sin changed nudity to nakedness. What they had seen before as normal and beautiful they now saw as abnormal and dirty.

Sin has clouded the issues, twisted the light rays, distorted the facts, and changed the attitudes. It has affected both the 'seeing mechanisms and the understanding mechanisms. Because of sin, we see things much differently than we would if we had no sin.

Needed: A Divine Ophthalmologist

Ophthalmology, according to a dictionary definition, is "a medical specialty encompassing the anatomy, functions, pathology, and treatment of the eye."

Just as the physical eye needs a specialist, so the spiritual eye needs a specialist.

It needs a specialist who can diagnose the problem, prescribe a remedy, and initiate the healing process.

A spiritual problem needs a spiritual remedy and a divine healer. In short, a Divine Ophthalmologist.

In the next chapter we'll probe more deeply into the subject of blindness, but now let's look briefly at what Christ can do.

Keith Miller gets the title of his famous book, *The Second Touch*, from the story of Jesus' healing of the blind man, as recorded in Mark 8:22-25:

> They came to Bethsaida, and some people brought a blind man and begged Jesus to touch him. He took the blind man by the hand and led him outside the village. When he had spit on the man's eyes and put his hands on him, Jesus asked, "Do you see anything?"
>
> He looked up and said, "I see people; they look like trees walking around."
>
> Once more Jesus put his hands on the man's eyes. Then his eyes were opened, his sight was restored, and he saw everything clearly.

Jesus was not content merely to enable the man to see

light and dim forms. He was not satisfied to leave him with blurred vision. He wanted to heal the man completely. So Jesus applied the "second touch," enabling him to see everything clearly.

That's the kind of ophthalmologist Jesus is in the spiritual sense as well. First he clears up our basic blindness, by enabling us to see the light. Then he begins working on the fine points of good vision.

When Jesus heals us of our blindness, we see the light. Our sight is restored. That is the basic, fundamental miracle. But this does not mean we then can see perfectly. Our mental and spiritual vision may yet be faulty. Jesus is not done with us yet; there is much, much more that He wishes to do with our eyes. He treats our nearsightedness, our farsightedness, our color-blindness, and other maladies which afflict us. He removes the specks and dirt, enabling us to see things undistinguishable to the untreated eye. His divine ophthalmology is a lifelong process.

As we grow in our faith, our ability to see will improve. The sanctification process will influence our perceptive powers.

"So from now on we regard no one from a worldly point of view. Though we once regarded Christ in this way, we do so no longer. Therefore, if anyone is in Christ, he is a new creation; the old has gone, the new has come!" (2 Corinthians 5:16,17).

According to this magnificent verse, Christ changes our point of view. We don't look at things in the same way as we looked at them before. God has performed the miracle of a "new creation" in our lives, and this inner change affects our outlook, in two directions. The way we look at others: "So from now on we regard no one from a worldly point of view" (v. 16).

The way we look at Christ: "Though we once regarded Christ in this way, we do so no longer" (v. 16).

The chapters of this book will explore some of the ways in which the Divine Ophthalmologist works with us to improve our vision. I use the phrase *with us*, because He provides power and direction, but He also needs our cooperation. Improving the eyesight is a divine-human project, God's working with us and our working with God.

May the Lord open our eyes that we may behold wondrous things out of His Word.

Eye Exercises

That Will Enhance Your Spiritual Perception

1. Memorize each of the "Eye Drops" in this chapter and in the subsequent chapters as well. We realize that Bible memorization isn't very popular any more, but there is no better way to keep God's Word before you than by committing it to memory. Suggestion: Write each of these verses on a three-by-five-inch index card. On the other side of each card write the Scripture reference. Read through the cards every morning, and carry them with you throughout the day in your purse or billfold. Use odd moments throughout the day, as when waiting for a traffic light or waiting in line, to engage in a memory drill.

2. Read some interesting and informative material on the anatomy and physiology of the eye. You will find good material in library books and encyclopedias. You will be impressed by the intricate and loving majesty of God that is displayed in this small organ.

3. Bring to class some pictures that illustrate how both the eyes and the mind can play tricks on an individual. You might use some of the common optical illusions frequently shown to demonstrate this phenomenon. Or, you may be able to find photographs similar to the ones mentioned in this chapter (two-headed camel and huge man on boat).

4. Tonight, before going to sleep, pray for your eyes. Thank God for your physical eyes and ask Him to enable you to retain your eyesight. Thank God for your spiritual eyes as well, and ask Him to enable you to gain better spiritual perception.

Eye Drops

From the Divine Ophthalmologist

1. "So from now on we regard no one from a worldly point of view. Though we once regarded Christ in this way, we do so no longer. Therefore, if anyone is in Christ, he is a new creation; the old has gone, the new has come!"

2 Corinthians 5:16,17

2. "Once more Jesus put his hands on the man's eyes. Then his eyes were opened, his sight was restored, and he saw everything clearly."

Mark 8:25

3. "The eye is the lamp of the body. If your eyes are good, your whole body will be full of light. But if your eyes are bad, your whole body will be full of darkness. If then the light within you is darkness, how great is that darkness!"

Matthew 6:22

4. "Open my eyes, that I may behold wondrous things out of thy law."

Psalm 119:18

Chapter 2
Blindness
(Inability to See Spiritual Truth)

Physical Blindness

Blindness is a total or partial loss of the ability to see, the most serious of all the maladies of the eye.

There are degrees of blindness.

The person with *educational* blindness can distinguish light and darkness as well as many objects, but his ability to receive an education is impaired.

Vocational blindness prevents a person from continuing the kind of work he has been doing.

Economic blindness keeps him from doing any kind of work that requires the use of the eyes.

Total blindness is just what it says. The totally blind person cannot even distinguish light from darkness.

People are blinded in various ways. Some are blind from birth. Others are blinded later — by accident, disease, or war.

Blindness affects enough people to make it a major problem. And it isn't just a medical problem, either. Its repercussions spill over into sociology, psychology, and economics. It is estimated that in the United States alone 430,000 people are legally blind. It is estimated that, worldwide, there are 14 million blind people.

Besides being a major problem for the victims themselves, blindness affects the families, the schools, and the economy as a whole.

Spiritual Blindness

If millions of people in the world are physically blind, then many more millions are spiritually blind.

19

The spiritually blind person cannot understand spiritual things. He has a lack of sensitivity to the things that affect his soul.

He may be able to understand the most complicated of mathematical theorems. but he cannot understand what God is all about. He may be well aware of physical needs, but he is completely unaware of his spiritual needs. He sees himself as body and mind; but not as body, mind, and spirit.

Jesus said that those who failed to understand His parables were a fulfillment of Isaiah's prophecy: "You will be ever hearing but never understanding; you will be ever seeing, but never perceiving" (Matthew 13:14). The disciples, on the other hand, could understand: "But blessed are your eyes because they see, and your ears because they hear" (Matthew 13:16).

When Jesus wept over Jerusalem he cried out, "If you, even now, had only known on this day what would bring you peace — but now it is hidden from your eyes" (Luke 19:42).

There is even some wry humor in this matter of blindness. Isaiah talks about blind watchmen (Isaiah 56:10), and Jesus called the Pharisees blind guides. "If a blind man leads a blind man, both will fall into a pit" (Matthew 15:14).

The lukewarm church of Laodicea was unaware of its poor spiritual condition. It believed it was rich, prosperous, and strong, but instead it was "wretched, pitiful, poor, blind, and naked" (Revelation 3:17). The Holy Spirit said to it, "I counsel you to buy from me . . . salve to put on your eyes, so you can see" (v. 18).

Some Examples of Spiritual Sight and Spiritual Blindness

1. When Elisha's servant, Gehazi, went out early in the morning, he was terrified to see the city surrounded by the horses and chariots of the Syrians.

"Alas, my master! What shall we do?" he cried.

"Fear not," said Elisha, "for those who are with us are more than those who are against us."

Then he prayed that the young man's eyes would be opened. And the Lord opened the eyes of Gehazi, and he saw that the mountain was full of horses and chariots of fire around Elisha. (See 2 Kings 6:15-23.)

Spiritual sight.

2. The prophet Jeremiah called to his countrymen,
"Hear this, O foolish and senseless people,
who have eyes, but see not,
who have ears, but hear not" (5:21).
Spiritual blindness.

3. Philip the evangelist approached the chariot on the Gaza road and discovered that its Ethiopian occupant was reading from the scroll of Isaiah.

"Do you understand what you are reading?" asked Philip.

"How can I, unless someone explains it to me?" replied the man.

Philip climbed into the chariot with him, and as they rode on, he explained how the prophecy was fulfilled by Jesus of Nazareth.

After some time they came to some water, and the Ethiopian said, "Look, here is water. Why shouldn't I be baptized?" (See Acts 8:26-40.)

Spiritual sight.

3. Saul of Tarsus saw Jesus as an imposter. He believed that the new cult, Christianity, was a threat to the pure religion of the Jewish people.

On his way to Damascus to persecute the Christian believers he was struck blind by a bright flash of noonday light, and he blurted out, "Who are you, Lord?" (See Acts 9:1-10.)

Spiritual sight.

4. Evangelistic callers from a local church made a full presentation of the gospel to a new young couple in town, Tom and Marie Harris. They presented the biblical truth

21

about God, Jesus, sin, salvation, and faith. They paused periodically to ask questions like "Is that clear?" and "Do you understand?"

Tom and Marie replied, "Yes, we do."

Then one of the callers challenged Tom and Marie to accept Christ as Savior.

To which Tom replied, "What is the difference, really, between Episcopalians and Baptists?"

And Marie said, "Would you like some coffee and cake?"

Spiritual blindness.

5. Ann Kolar sang three or four solos at the evening service of the Faith Community Church in Stickney, Illinois, her guide dog snoozing quietly under the pew as she sang from the platform.

Everyone loved to hear Ann sing the old hymns. But it was her rendition of "The Light of the World is Jesus" that moved the worshipers most that night. When she got to "Once I was blind, but now I can see," there was hardly a dry eye in the place.

Spiritual sight.

6. Mary Tyler doesn't attend church any more, although she is a member. "I just don't get anything out of the sermon," she says, "and I haven't gotten around to going anywhere else. Maybe next year, when I have more time."

Spiritual blindness.

7. Mark Gilyard attended the evangelistic crusade because of intellectual and personal curiosity. As a graduate student in psychology he was interested in knowing what learning responses, motivational factors, and techniques of mass psychology were being used by the famous evangelist and his staff.

As the sermon progressed, Mark forgot about analyzing the crusade and began analyzing himself. He saw that his life was messed up; he saw that all his other attempts to find satisfaction had failed; he saw that what Christ had to offer made sense. When the invitation was given, Mark swallowed his scholarly pride and went forward.

Spiritual sight.

8. A seminary professor and a ninth grade boy find themselves seated next to each other in an airplane.

"Where are you going, son?" asks the professor.

"To Philadelphia," the youth answers, "to my grandfather's funeral."

"Please accept my sympathy. I'm sorry to hear that he died."

"We'll miss him. But he was 89 and had a lot of pain. He's happier now that he's in heaven."

"Do you really believe that, son?"

"Why, of course. Jesus rose from the dead, didn't He?"

"Well . . ."

"You believe it, don't you?"

"Let's put it this way. I believe that the disciples wanted to express in some way that the influence of Jesus would never die, so they used the myth of the resurrection to convey that idea."

"I still believe in the resurrection. Of Jesus and my grandpa."

Spiritual blindness and spiritual sight.

What do all these anecdotes have in common?

They all have something to do with the ability to see spiritual reality.

They deal with the kind of perceptiveness that goes beneath the surface of things; that probes into the depth of one's soul; that asks searching questions about one's relationship to God; that deals honestly with life after death.

Causes of Blindness

For physical blindness there is always a cause. It may be accident or disease or assault. For spiritual blindness there is also always a cause. There may be more, but here are three:

1. *Deliberate refusal to see*

"None are so blind," it has been said, "as those who will not see."

Jeremiah and Isaiah both spoke of those "who have eyes, but see not" (Isaiah 43:8; Jeremiah 5:21). Their optical equipment was there, but they refused to use it.

Said Jesus of those who did not comprehend the spiritual meaning of His parables: "They have closed their eyes. Otherwise they might see with their eyes" (Matthew 13:15).

Tom and Marie Harris understood the facts of the gospel, but they were unwilling to see what it had to do with them. So they closed their eyes and tried to get the callers sidetracked onto a less sensitive subject.

There are many reasons why some folks refuse to see. Perhaps they know that spiritual sight will bring a change in their life-style, and this they want to avoid at all costs. Perhaps they don't like the people who are trying to get them to see the truth. Perhaps they are simply set in their own ways.

Whatever the reason, it results in a deliberate closing of the eyes.

2. *Preoccupation with the material world*

Materialism was Gehazi's problem. He was preoccupied with the obvious. He didn't realize that beyond the material world there is a vast world of spiritual substance as well.

The tragic loss of the rich young ruler was due to his preoccupation with his possessions.

The rich farmer was so busy building barns that he forgot to build for eternity.

What the poet Wordsworth said is true today:

> The world is too much with us: late and soon,
> Getting and spending, we lay waste our powers.

Perhaps one reason why Ann Kolar could sing so boldly, "Once I was blind, but now I can see," was because her perception of the world of matter did not interfere with her perception of the world of Spirit.

Actually the things seen by the natural eye are the most

unreal, and the things seen by the spiritual eye are the most real. The Bible says, "What is seen is temporary, but what is unseen is eternal" (2 Corinthians 4:18).

Forget for a while, if you will, your businesses, boats, bills, buildings, budgets, brooms, brooches, and baseball games, and take time for a sunning session with your soul.

3. *Loss by atrophy*

Some, as we have said, refuse to see. Others are blind to truth because they are distracted. Still others cannot see because they have lost the capability of sight.

When our family visited the Mammoth Cave in Kentucky a few years ago, we saw pinkish, five-inch fish called blindfish. They had no eyes. Their species had lived so long in the darkness that they had lost their ability to see. We were told there are about twenty species of blind fish in the world, living in caves and in the deepest parts of the sea.

It is possible for that to happen to people. They can live so long in the darkness that they lose their ability to see. They can refuse to see the light for so long that even if they wish to see again, they cannot. The rods and cones of the spiritual retina become desensitized; the optic nerve of the spirit is blocked off by the cancerous growth of self. There is no possibility of perception until there takes place either radical surgery or miraculous healing.

First Corinthians 2:14 says, "The man without the Spirit does not accept the things that come from the Spirit of God, for they are foolishness to him, and he cannot understand them, because they are spiritually discerned."

The letter to the Romans says of those who did not glorify God or give thanks to Him that "their thinking became futile and their foolish hearts were darkened" (Romans 1:21). Therefore God "gave them over to a depraved mind" (1:28). And in Romans 11:8 it says "God gave them a spirit of stupor, eyes so that they could not see and ears so that they could not hear, to this very day."

In 2 Corinthians 4:4 the blame for blindness is laid at

the feet of Satan: "The god of this age has blinded the minds of unbelievers, so that they cannot see the light of the gospel of the glory of Christ, who is the image of God."

They don't see because they can't see.

Jesus Came to Cure Our Blindness

According to the prophets, one of the functions of the promised Messiah was to give sight to the blind.

> In that day the deaf shall hear
>   the words of a book,
> and out of their gloom and darkness
>   the eyes of the blind shall see.
>
> *Isaiah 29:18*

Jesus considered Himself the fulfillment of prophecies such as this, for in His inaugural sermon at Nazareth He read similar words from Isaiah 61 and said, "Today this scripture is fulfilled in your hearing" (Luke 4:21).

Jesus fulfilled this claim by healing many people who were physically blind.

But more than that, He fulfilled it by giving spiritual sight.

Through His teaching He cast fresh light upon the will of the Father.

Through His earthly ministry He enabled us to see more clearly the love of the Father.

Through His death He lit a floodlight on the path that leads to heaven.

Through His Holy Spirit He enabled us to grasp the significance of it all and to receive it for ourselves.

Said Jesus, "For judgment I have come into this world, so that the blind will see and those who see will turn out to be blind" (John 9:39). He is speaking here of those who will respond favorably to His offer of salvation and those who will reject it. Some who were spiritually blind will be given spiritual sight. On the other hand, those who thought themselves to be spiritually enlightened will, by their disbelief in Christ, become spiritually blind.

As hopeless as the problem may sometimes seem, something fortunately can be done about spiritual blindness. We suggest a three-step treatment.

1. *Seek the light.*

After Philip had been invited to follow Jesus, he went immediately to his friend Nathanael and said to him, "We have found the one Moses wrote about in the Law, and about whom the prophets also wrote — Jesus of Nazareth, the son of Joseph."

Nathanael was skeptical — perhaps because of the many impostors who had claimed to be the Messiah.

"Nazareth! Can anything good come from there?" he cracked.

"Come and see," said Philip.

Despite his skepticism, Nathanael came to see. He squelched his doubts and decided to give it a try. Although he did so suspiciously and hesitantly, he opened his eyes. (See John 1:43-51.)

He came, he saw, and he believed. His blindness was overcome. But first he had to be *willing* to see.

Then Jesus promised Nathanael he would see a great deal more: "I tell you the truth, you shall all see heaven open, and the angels of God ascending and descending on the Son of Man" (John 1:51).

Young Mark Gilyard, who attended the evangelistic crusade out of intellectual curiosity, would never have found Christ had he not come to see for himself. He would never admit it, of course, but we suspect that unconsciously he came seeking for an answer. Deep in his soul he wanted to know the content of the evangelist's message, not just his technique.

The Ethiopian on the Gaza road, though blind to the real meaning of the prophecy, was seeking. He was looking for an answer. And he found it.

"Seek the Lord while he may be found, call upon him

while he is near," invited the prophet (Isaiah 55:6).

And Jesus said, "Seek and you will find" (Matthew 7:7).

2. *Experience the miracle of the new birth.*

Blindness usually cannot be cured, even by surgery. It takes nothing short of a miracle for the blind person to be able to see again.

A miracle must also take place before we can see spiritual truth. God must perform an act of restoration on the seeing apparatus of the soul.

Jesus said to Nicodemus, who came by night seeking the light (remember no. 1 above?), "I tell you the truth, unless a man is born again, he cannot see the kingdom of God" (John 3:3).

According to Jesus, a miracle is exactly what can take place to restore our spiritual sight.

God can take the sightless, blind eyes of the soul and enable them to see the love He has for us.

God can take the stubborn pride of spiritual blindness and enable us to see the desperate need we have for forgiveness and cleansing.

God can take eyes encrusted with the cataracts of skepticism and enable them to see the deep meaning of Christ's hanging on the cross.

God can take the optic nerve of the soul that has been blocked off by the cancer of sin and can remove the malignancy in such a way that the nerve is open and alive again.

God can take the pupil of the soul that has been enflamed with hate and vindictiveness and can bathe it in the tears of love.

God can take the retina of the heart that has been enflamed by lust and greed and can reduce the swelling to the point that it can see the pure and happy life He has in mind for us.

God can take away the iris clouded with despair and hopelessness and enable us to see the life eternal he has prepared for all who believe in Him.

God can take the muscles of the eyes that are just too

weary to go on moving for another day and can give them new life, vitality, and power.

In short — when the new birth takes place, the eyes of the soul are opened to comprehend that (1) we are sinful and hopelessly lost, (2) Jesus died on the cross to pay the penalty for our sins, (3) Jesus rose from the dead to lead the way to eternal life, and (4) by believing in Him we can obtain forgiveness of our sins and the promise of eternal life.

3. *Believe on Jesus Christ.*

A little later in that same conversation with Nicodemus, Jesus said of Himself that "whoever believes in him shall not perish but have everlasting life" (John 3:16). And still later He said, "Whoever puts his faith in the Son has eternal life, but whoever rejects the Son will not see that life, for God's wrath remains on him" (v. 36).

It would seem, according to this, that our belief, along with the miracle of the new birth, is necessary for the restoration of spiritual sight. It is our faith that enables us to see eternal life. It is through eyes gazing upon Jesus Christ in trust that we receive all His benefits.

Theologians have debated for years about which comes first — belief in Jesus Christ or the miracle of the new birth. Good arguments can be made on either side.

It's mysterious. It's like the chicken and the egg.

But really — isn't it more important to get on with raising chickens than it is to argue forever whether the chicken or the egg came first?

It is safe to say that the exact sequence is understood fully only by God in His supreme intelligence.

What is supremely important to us is that we know and do our part. The new birth is passive; it is something God does for us. Belief is active; it is something we do toward God. Therefore the responsibility for belief rests upon us. We are nowhere told to just sit around and wait for God to regenerate us. We are exhorted, commanded, and pleaded with to believe.

Only after we believe and look back upon our experience can we understand that God was actively at work in us all along, giving us the new birth and regenerating us from the inside. Then we can see that even our faith is a gift of God. It's all a part of that marvelous interaction of the human and the divine.

The important thing is to have faith. To believe. To trust. To receive. Now.

Then you can say with Ann Kolar, "Once I was blind, but now I can see. The light of the world is Jesus."

Eye Exercises

For Blindness

1. Pray today for a blind person. Then do something for someone who is blind. Perhaps he needs some Braille books from the library. Perhaps he would like to listen to good cassette tapes owned by the church.

2. Thank God for the ability to see. It's strange, isn't it — how we praise God for one miracle of healed blindness, while taking for granted the good sight of thousands who need no healing.

3. Pray today for someone who is spiritually blind, who has so far resisted all the appeals of the gospel. Is there something you can do to make it easier for him to see? Is there a personal testimony you can share, or a book that would be worth his while to read?

4. Do *you* have the kind of sight it takes for entrance into the kingdom of God? Do you understand what Christ did for you, and what you must do in response? If matters are still unclear, talk to a pastor or a trusted Christian friend. Read the Bible and some outstanding Christian books. The point is, *seek*. Then you will find.

Eye Drops

For the Prevention and Cure of Blindness

1. "Blessed are your eyes because they see, and your ears because they hear."

Matthew 13:16

2. "I counsel you to buy from me . . . salve to put on your eyes, so you can see."

Revelation 3:18

3. "The man without the Spirit does not accept the things that come from the Spirit of God, for they are foolishness to him, and he cannot understand them, because they are spiritually discerned."

1 Corinthians 2:14

4. "Seek and you will find."

Matthew 7:7

Chapter 3
Myopia
(Nearsightedness)

my·o·pi·a (mī-ō′pē-a) n.   1. *Pathology*. A visual defect in which distant objects appear blurred because their images are focused in front of the retina rather than on it; nearsightedness. 2. Shortsightedness or lack of discernment in thinking or planning: *For Lorca, New York is a symbol of spiritual myopia, where man . . . has lost sight of those elemental natural forces"* (Edwin Honig).

Have you ever looked through Aunt Jenny's photo album? The one with the pictures she took when they made that trip out West?

You remember, I'm sure, that memorable photograph of Uncle Herman standing in front of Mount Rushmore. At least you thought it was Mount Rushmore: Uncle Herman was in sharper focus than anyone really wanted him to be, but George Washington and Abraham Lincoln could very well have been Jackie Gleason and Grandma Moses.

Then there was that close-up of a chipmunk on a rail fence in Yellowstone National Park. You can see every buttercup on the hill behind the fence, but the chipmunk looks like a blob of hash brown potatoes.

The problem with Aunt Jenny's pictures may have been her $25.95 plastic-lens camera. Or, the problem may have been Aunt Jenny herself, who was concentrating so hard on not getting her finger in front of the lens that she forgot to set the focus properly.

Ordinarily one's eyes focus much better than Aunt Jenny's camera. In fact, they work much better than Uncle Herman's $495 camera, which he carries around in a huge leather bag slung across his shoulders along with an astounding assortment of lenses, meters, and mysterious black attachments.

You are now looking at the words in this sentence. You are focusing on an object about twelve inches from your eyes. The words are in focus, are they not?

Now look up quickly and gaze out the window. Now you're back again. What did you see? A house down the street, or a bird in the sky, or a distant hill? And did you not see them as distinctly as you see these words?

What a marvelous miracle is the eye! Automatically, smoothly, effortlessly, and unconsciously the lenses in your eyes changed focus from the near to the far and back again to the near. No camera lens, no matter how expensive and complex, can work quite like that.

But once in a while the intricate focusing mechanism of the eye does not work properly. The light rays may, for instance, meet in front of the retina instead of on it. As a result, the person has myopia, or nearsightedness. He can see objects clearly if they are nearby, but he sees them fuzzily if they are at a distance.

Nearsighted Mr. Parker holds his evening newspaper six inches from his nose.

Nearsighted Mrs. Mobbelsdorf almost sticks herself in the eye with a needle when she tries to thread it.

Nearsighted Jimmy Jones parks himself a foot away from the television set, and everyone else yells at him to move.

Some persons have the opposite problem — hyperopia, or farsightedness. They can see things clearly if they are far away, but cannot see objects close by. Hyperopia is the subject of the next chapter.

Most of us were farsighted when we were born: our eyes were too short for good focus. During childhood our eyes began to get longer, and the process should have been completed during adolescence. With some, however, the eyes continued to elongate, causing the rays of light to be focused on a point in front of the retina rather than on it.

This process can take place rather rapidly, causing a noticeable change of vision within six months to a year. Once puberty is passed, little change of this kind takes place.

It is estimated that between 20 percent and 30 percent of the adult population is affected to some extent by nearsightedness. Many, of course, are not aware of it, since they take blurred vision for granted.

Both myopia and hyperopia can be problems with the nonphysical eyes as well. The focus of the eyes may be 20/20, but the focus of life may be badly distorted.

We now consider some of the symptoms and cures for nearsightedness. Remember, myopia causes us to see clearly what is close at hand, but makes indistinct what is far away.

Two Classic Cases of Myopia

One of the most remarkable cases of myopia in history is recorded in Genesis 25:29-34.

Esau, the he-man, hairy-chested, outdoor type, came in from hunting one day, and he was hungry. And when Esau was hungry, he was *really* hungry.

Who should be preparing the meal but Jacob, the soft-skinned, mama's favorite, homebody type.

"Let me eat some of that red pottage, for I am famished!" roared Esau.

"First sell me your birthright," Jacob said.

"I am about to die; of what use is a birthright to me?" bellowed the hairy one.

So he sold his double portion of inheritance — sheep, goats, cattle, tents, and the rest of his father's possessions — for a loaf of bread and a bowl of stew.

The cause of this unbelievable transaction? Myopia.

Esau was able to focus his eyes on the bowl of stew, but he seemed incapable of focusing them on the inheritance.

He could concentrate on the immediate, but not on the eventual.

The present was in focus, but the future was fuzzy.

His loss of perspective was so acute that he was fooled into thinking a hot stew was more important than his father's flocks.

Myopia, then, is far more than a case of bad eyesight. It can cause notoriously bad judgment.

Faulty perceptions lead to faulty suppositions.

Fuzzy seeing causes fuzzy thinking.

An even more tragic incident is found in Jesus' conversation with a rich young ruler, as recorded in Luke 18:18-26.

The young man came to Jesus, asking, "Good teacher, what must I do to inherit eternal life?" (v. 18).

This man had a lot of things going for him. He had (a) youth, (b) riches, (c) power, (d) good morals, and (e) an inquiring mind. Yet he realized something wasn't quite right.

Jesus diagnosed the problem immediately: myopia.

He saw that the young man's eyes were so fixed on his possessions, he couldn't see beyond them. He was simply unable to focus on anything else. What he owned had become the passion of his life.

So Jesus, the Great Physician, prescribed radical surgery: "Sell everything you have and give it to the poor, and you will have treasure in heaven. Then come, follow me" (v. 22).

Note that Jesus was not saying good works would save him. He could be saved only by following Jesus in faith. But in this case something was making it impossible to take even the first step of faith — his possessions.

Unfortunately his myopia was terminal. The man found it impossible to lift his eyes and focus on the footsteps of Jesus. "He became very sad, because he was a man of great wealth" (v. 23).

Overcome Myopia by Seeking for a Vision

The Bible says, "All we like sheep have gone astray; we have turned every one to his own way" (Isaiah 53:6). This implies that we can be nearsighted in the same way sheep are nearsighted. Sheep are not distinguished by their brilliance in the animal world. A sheep will put his head down and concentrate only on the grass in front of his nose; he will move from one tuft to another without looking up, without checking directions, caring only for the next mouthful of food. Soon he may lose himself in a thicket or gully, having wandered away from the others.

It's possible to live all of life this way — drifting along without particular goals, doing what comes naturally, taking each day at a time, satisfying one's immediate hungers, and hoping for the best; but moving according to no game plan, believing not much of anything, never stopping to check directions.

Yet God says, "Where there is no vision, the people perish" (Proverbs 29:18 KJV).

God wants us to rise above the level of the animal, who lives only by instinct. The Bible teaches "that man does not live by bread alone, but that man lives by everything that proceeds out of the mouth of the Lord" (Deuteronomy 8:3).

God has a plan for the life of each of us. He wants us to use His blueprint to build a castle of precious stones, not a tarpaper shack.

He wants us to raise our heads occasionally from the next tuft of grass to check where we are going.

He wants us to be pilgrims traveling toward the Holy City, not hobos wandering from one seedy burg to the other.

He wants us to be tourists consulting a road map, not just wanderers following the highway that seems widest.

He wants us to be adventurers occasionally scaling the cliffs to get a breath-taking view from the height, not just lostlings hacking our way through the dense underbrush.

God wants us to check our ship's position by the North Star, not just to sail in circles on an uncharted sea.

They called the steamboat "Fulton's Folly" and they called Alaska "Seward's Icebox," but Robert Fulton had a vision and Secretary of State William H. Seward had a vision.

It is men and women of vision who have made America what it is today. They are the ones who saw beyond the immediate moment, the immediate need, and the immediate place.

Every great piece of literature is based on great vision. Every great painting, every great sculpture, every great symphony, every great marketing plan, every great football game, every great mousetrap has been preceded by a vision.

Woe to the generation that does not have its visionaries who can lift their heads in faith from the next tuft of grass and catch a glimpse of greater things ahead.

Overcome Myopia by Looking Beyond the Immediate Pain

God has created our human nervous system with a marvelous, yet disconcerting ability to call attention to our troubles. The nerve endings literally scream out their message of agony and pain.

The sky may be blue, the breezes balmy, and the flowers beautiful, but if you've got a throbbing toothache you hardly notice any of them.

Your party may be a bubbling success, your friends may be pleasant, and the conversation may be scintillating; but it's all a blurred cloud of sound if you're worried about the grandchild with the 105-degree fever.

In fact, we may develop a myopia that throws us into a deep depression.

We may begin to concentrate so completely on our ills that we fail to see our blessings.

Our eyes may become so downcast that we forget to lift them to see the light.

We may focus so intently on the perils that we ignore the possibilities.

We may gaze upon the dirt and fail to perceive the divine.

We may focus on that which is seen, forgetting that the unseen even exists.

Paul had a word for those who find themselves in such a myopic plight: "Our light and momentary troubles are achieving for us an eternal glory that far outweighs them all. So we fix our eyes not on what is seen, but on what is unseen. For what is seen is temporary, but what is unseen is eternal" (2 Corinthians 4:17, 18).

Notice how the Bible here urges us to change our focus. We are to see that the present trouble is "light," "momentary," and "temporary"; the future experience, "eternal" and "glory."

The love and grace of God do not always brightly glow in obvious splendor. Sometimes they are, as the verse says, "unseen." But ultimately they are the only real and lasting things. Therefore we can fix our eyes upon them, rather than upon our troubles. If we do this we may be able to say with the writer, "We are hard pressed on every side, but not crushed; perplexed, but not in despair; persecuted, but not abandoned; struck down, but not destroyed" (2 Corinthians 4:8, 9).

*Combat Myopia by Focusing on the
Needs of Others Far Away as Well as
Our Own Needs Right Here*

As Esau so aptly illustrated, it's dreadfully easy to be nearsighted. Our immediate needs literally cry out in our ears, while the screams of distant needs seem like the wind whistling through the pines.

It's easy to focus on our feet; it's not so easy to focus on the horizon.

Out of sight, out of mind, says the proverb.

It's not hard to see that our children need a house, clothing, and three meals a day — to say nothing of a doll, a train, a tricycle, a baseball bat, a bike, a radio, a portable TV, a motorcycle, a pink telephone with a private number, movie tickets, jewelry, encyclopedias, guitar lessons, contact lenses, and braces on the teeth.

But it's more difficult to focus on the bloated bellies of Bangladesh; the kids playing with a stick and an old tire in an alley in Chicago; seven children sleeping on one urine-soaked coverless mattress in Kentucky; and the children left homeless and orphaned by an earthquake in South America.

It's easy to perceive the needs of our local church while ignoring the needs of the church far away. Take the case of Andrew H., deacon at First Church of Hickory Hills. Mr. H. makes a good living as an insurance agent and gives nearly 8 percent of his income to the church. This places him high on the "good givers" list. Hence his views on church spending are highly regarded. Last month one of the other deacons suggested that since the church income is now $92,000 per year, the budget for missions should be increased from $4,000 to $8,000. Deacon H. strongly objected, saying things like "Charity begins at home" and "I think we ought to be setting money aside for a new pipe organ."

It's not difficult for a man to see his own need for a new set of golf clubs, a new drill press, a night out with the boys, and more frequent sex experiences.

It's not difficult for a woman to see her own need for an automatic dishwasher, an electronic organ, a new spring wardrobe, and more communication with her husband.

But it's more difficult for each to see the needs of the other. The eyes tend to be nearsighted when it comes to our personal needs and desires.

Jesus prescribed an excellent treatment for this kind of myopia. He prescribed *love for all*.

" 'Love the Lord your God with all your heart, with all your soul and with all your mind.' This is the first and greatest commandment. And the second is like it: 'Love your neighbor as yourself' " (Matthew 22:37-39).

Notice please, that love always focuses on someone else.

It can focus on God ("Love the Lord your God . . .").
It can focus on others ("Love your neighbor . . . ").
It can focus on yourself (". . . as yourself ").

The love Jesus prescribes is not a love blind to ourselves or our families. But it is also a love that dares to look up and out — up to God and out to the world.

This kind of charity doesn't begin at home. It begins at God, then travels to the home and to the world.

This kind of love isn't always easy. It takes an act of the will, a deliberate decision of the mind. It takes concentration to overcome nearsightedness.

Don't imagine for a minute that the Samaritan traveler in Jesus' parable didn't have to cope with myopia: "This man is a Jew. Charity begins at home. What will people think? Perhaps those robbers are still here, hiding behind that rock. I'm already behind in my schedule. I'm no medical doctor."

But the man from Samaria overcame whatever nearsighted thoughts he may have had. He stopped, treated the man's wounds with olive oil, took him on his own donkey to the nearest inn, and paid the expenses himself.

Those who heard this parable of Jesus understood what He was saying: The neighbor you ought to love isn't limited to the nice guy next door.

Jesus said, "Therefore go and make disciples of all nations" (Matthew 28:19).

The word is *all*. Not *some*. Not *white*. Not *nearby*. The word is *all*.

The Book of Acts records these further words of Jesus: "And you will be my witnesses in Jerusalem, and in all Judea and Samaria, and to the ends of the earth" (1:8).

Evangelism begins at home, but it doesn't end there. Our loving concern for the world cannot be nearsighted.

Eye Exercises

For the Prevention and Cure of Myopia

1. Discipline yourself to read an article about missions

in your denominational magazine. Read it from beginning to end, concentrating on what you are reading. After you have read it, pause to pray about what you have read. Then, after praying, ask yourself, "What can I do about it?" Then do it.

2. Consider initiating a "Missions Sunday" once a month in your Sunday school. It can combat mission myopia in three ways:

    (a) by educating pupils about missions
    (b) by raising money for missions
    (c) by inspiring pupils to become missionaries

You may wish to select a different project each month, introducing the subject with a filmstrip, film, mounted photographs, or a talk.

3. On a sheet of paper list five or more goals you wish to reach within the next ten years. These may be in such areas as money, hobbies, education, work, family, love, religion, and service. Be bold and creative. Don't be afraid of a vision. Call out some of those secret yearnings which you never thought were possible to achieve.

4. Examine your life to see if you are trading your birthright for a bowl of stew. In other words, are you fixing your eyes on some immediate, trivial object, while spurning a long-range, magnificent blessing?

Some possible bad trades:

    (a) A car — for a college education.
    (b) A hasty marriage — for a good marriage.
    (c) Extra income — for being home with the family.
    (d) Sunday work — for worship at church.

Eye Drops

*Bible Verses Which, If Applied Properly,
Will Do Wonders for Myopia*

1. "Where there is no vision, the people perish."
Proverbs 29:18 KJV

2. "Therefore go and make disciples of all nations."

Matthew 28:19

3. "Our light and momentary troubles are achieving for us an eternal glory that far outweighs them all. So we fix our eyes not on what is seen, but on what is unseen. For what is seen is temporary, but what is unseen is eternal."

2 Corinthians 4:17,18

4. "Where your treasure is, there your heart will be also."

Matthew 6:21

Chapter 4
Hyperopia
(Farsightedness)

hy·per·o·pi·a (hī′pər ō′pe-ə) n.   A pathological condition of the eye in which parallel rays are focused behind the retina because of a refractive error, or because of flattening of the globe of the eye, so that vision is better for distant than near objects. Also called "hypermetropia," "farsightedness," "long-sightedness."

Grandpa Miller won't admit it, of course, but he has hyperopia. He is farsighted.

He doesn't think he needs glasses. He can see perfectly well when he is driving, taking a walk to the post office, or watching television. The only time he has trouble is when he is reading a newspaper or a book. The reason is, of course, that "the printers are using smaller print to save paper." His children tell him he must either be tested for eyeglasses or get extensions for his arms.

Actually most of us were hyperopiacs when we were born. Our eyes were too short for a good focus. At about the age of six or seven our eyes began to elongate. By adolescence the process should have completed itself.

For some, however, the eyes are just too enthusiastic about growing up, and they keep on getting longer, causing myopia (nearsightedness).

For others the eyes never get quite long enough. The image is focused at a point behind the retina. The retina intercepts the light rays before they are focused, resulting in a blurred image. The result is permanent hyperopia.

Between one fourth and third of all adults have enough hyperopia to require help. They may not realize it, simply because they don't do much reading — now that television provides every evening's entertainment.

Others may wish to read, but get discouraged because their eyes get tired. The ciliary muscles must work extra hard to get the words in focus. Eventually these muscles need rest, and the farsighted person must look away for a time.

The farsighted person can see distant objects clearly, but has trouble with objects close by. It's as with the first photographs I took with my first inexpensive camera. I imagined myself to be a master photographer, carefully framing a distant mountain with the branches of a nearby oak tree. The finished photo showed a very handsome mountain, but the leaves of the nearby oak tree were like black fuzzballs. That's the way things look to a farsighted person.

You and I may or may not be troubled by the farsightedness of the physical eyes. But the chances are good that at one time or another we will be bothered by another kind of farsightedness — *the farsightedness that perceives clearly what is distant but fails to see what is close at hand.*

The hyperopic person has trouble focusing on the immediate, even though the eventual seems to be quite clear. The future seems well in hand, but the present poses insurmountable difficulties. Great goals are no problem, but immediate responsibilities are. Magnificent dreams are savored, but mundane tasks are avoided.

Let's examine some cures for certain strains of hyperopia.

Overcome Hyperopia by Seeing
Present Opportunities as Well as
Eventual Goals

Do you imagine yourself becoming a renowned writer, being asked to autograph books and to appear on television talk shows, and having your old grade-school play-mates say of you, "I played on the merry-go-round with her when we were kids together back in Hickok Corners" — but when you sit down to write the first draft of a short story, you get up to make coffee, then remember to water the plants, then gaze out of the window for a while, and finally go for a ride to pick up the groceries?

If you do, you've got hyperopia.

There is only one cure. Sit down at the typewriter and start typing. No matter if it doesn't sound like Shakespeare or even Jacqueline Susann, or if it doesn't make any sense at all. The only way to write is to write.

Do you plan someday to become a famous surgeon, in demand by all the celebrities for their operations, charging fantastic fees that people are more than delighted to pay, seeing your name in the medical textbooks as having developed a new technique for operating on gall bladders — but instead of studying six hours for the big chemistry test you spend three hours watching television, two and a half hours playing Ping-Pong, and one half-hour quickly reviewing your notes?

If so, you've got hyperopia.

There is only one cure. Sit down *now* and start studying. There is no easy path to greatness. The fulfillment of any of any of those dreams means thousands and thousands of hours of highly concentrated work, without the benefit of table tennis or television.

Do you hope some day to become the fashion plate of the neighborhood, coming out at every party with a new gown, being interviewed and photographed by the social editor of the local newspaper, and being asked to be a consultant at a benefit style show sponsored by the Booster's Club — but when your husband comes home from work you meet him with rollers in your hair and a 1957 vintage brownish flannel gown which you threw on at the last minute because all your other clothes were still in the hamper, waiting to be washed and ironed?

If you do, you've got hyperopia.

You can see the long-range glory, but are somehow missing the short-range opportunity. A good treatment for this type of hyperopia is to begin *today* to look neat, fresh, clean, and beautiful for those you love.

Do you imagine the day when you can contribute large sums of money to your church, paying for the new carpeting all by yourself, or supporting a missionary, or giving a challenge gift for the new building fund, pledging to match all other contributions received — but at the same time you are giving only 3 percent of your income to the Lord's work and are annoyed by the stewardship callers, telling them you will give what you can but don't want to be committed to any certain amount?

If you do, you've got hyperopia.

The cure is to begin *next Sunday* to give a more generous percentage of your income, no matter how small that income may be.

The list could go on and on —

— the farmer who envisions owning and operating a thousand acres, but keeps finding excuses for not getting his chores done;

— the young man who keeps promising his wife a new home and a better neighborhood, but can't keep a job more than six months at a time;

— the woman who sees the pot of gold at the end of the rainbow, but not the weeds in her own backyard;

— the minister who envisions himself preaching to vast multitudes, but who doesn't get out and make sick calls.

There is a most intriguing verse in Proverbs 17:

> A man of understanding sets his face toward wisdom, but the eyes of a fool are on the ends of the earth.
>
> *Proverbs 17:24*

Jesus also had something to say to those who expect to do great things for Him in the future. He said, "Do you not say, 'Four months more and then the harvest'? I tell you, open your eyes and look at the fields. They are ripe for harvest" (John 4:35).

Young person: It is a fine thing to look forward to the day you will become a minister or missionary. But why wait? Get your eyes in focus and see all whom you can witness to *now*.

Church member: Are you planning to become part of an evangelism calling program next year? Fine! But why wait till then? The harvest is ripe *now*. Don't look only to the future. Look to the present.

Overcome Hyperopia by Making Present Applications as Well as Believing in Great Principles

Do you claim, when with a minister friend, that you are in favor of full civil rights for all people, including blacks, and that you are a personal friend of a number of very fine black people, and that you believe we are all God's children and that Christ died for the whole world, and you give generously for missions in Africa — but you call the 40-year-old black teller at the bank a "boy," and you neglect to give any money for the inner-city work in your own city, and you treat a black saleswoman with less respect than you do a white saleswoman, and you object strongly when a black person applies for membership in your church?

If you do, you've got hyperopia.

The only cure is to talk less about great principles and to do more about immediate applications.

Do you advocate the principles of Jesus Christ, and believe that all believers ought to be witnesses for Him, and that we all ought to love one another as Christ loved us, and that the church is the body of Christ in which each member contributes to the upbuilding of the whole, and that Christians can have a great time together singing, sympathizing, and sharing — but at home you are a crotchety grump, and to your child's schoolteacher you are a chronic complainer, and to the checkout girl you are

47

a scowler, and to your neighbor's dog you are a creature to be avoided?

If you are, you've got hyperopia.

The only cure is to begin now to put the principles into action — at home, at your child's school, at the checkout counter, and in the company of your neighbor's dog.

Do you believe that changes in the social structure are necessary, and that you should be active in Americans for United Action, Concerned Citizens for Penal Reform, Committee to Keep Youths off the Street, the Caucus for the Study of Care for the Aged, the PSAAC, the TUUCW, the LOOPE, and the THUUD — but seldom are around to be with your own children, and never have time to visit your mother in the home for the aged, or write your sister whose husband is in jail?

If so, you suffer from hyperopia.

The letter by James is largely a handbook on how to cure farsightedness. It advocates *action* as well as *announcements*; it calls for *performance* as well as *principles*.

> Do not merely listen to the word, and so deceive yourselves. Do what it says (1:22).
>
> If anyone considers himself religious and yet does not keep a tight rein on his tongue, he deceives himself and his religion is worthless (1:26).
>
> What good is it, my brothers, if a man claims to have faith but has no deeds? (2:14).
>
> Suppose a brother or sister is without clothes and daily food. If one of you says to him, "Go, I wish you well; keep warm and well fed," but does nothing about his physical needs, what good is it? (2:15,16).
>
> You believe that there is one God. Good! Even the demons believe that — and shudder (2:19).
>
> Who is wise and understanding among you? Let him show it by his good life, by deeds done in the humility that comes from wisdom (3:13).
>
> Now listen, you who say, "Today or tomorrow we will go to this or that city, spend a year there, carry on business and make money." Why, you do not even know what will happen tomorrow (4:13).

In every case God, speaking through the author, is calling us to see clearly the responsibilities and opportunities which are right before our eyes, on our own doorsteps, at the present moment, right here and now.

He is not disparaging great faith or great vision or great principles. But he is saying that truly great faith, truly great vision, and truly great principles are those that are translated into action. They cannot exist long in a vacuum. They will generate activity, or they will evaporate like the morning mist.

It's possible that the good Samaritan may later have called up his congressman to advocate better police protection along Jericho Road and gone on a speaking tour calling for better relationships between Samaritans and Jews — but the first thing he did was to pour oil into the wounds of the injured man and take him to an inn.

Prevent Hyperopia by Enjoying the Present

I read not too long ago of a psychologist who surveyed 3,000 people for their attitudes on past, present, and future. He found that 90 percent of them were reminiscing about the past, anticipating the future, and enduring the present.

Youth were looking forward to getting a car, graduating, and getting married. Young marrieds were looking forward to children and financial security. Middle marrieds were looking forward to getting their children out of the house. Older marrieds were looking forward to retirement. Many of the old folks were actually looking forward to dying. But very few seemed to be relishing the present moment. Their farsightedness was blurring the joys of the present and near-at-hand.

There's a slogan appearing on wall posters: "When Walking Along the Path of Life, Pause to Smell the Flowers Along the Way."

That's good advice. Don't just look to the end of the trail.

When walking to the store for a half-gallon of milk (when was the last time you *walked* to the store?), look around you and you'll be surprised by what you see. Children playing on their tricycles. Cloud formations. A cat stalking something in the bushes. Flowers. With bees. An elderly couple, obviously just married. A little boy with ice cream from ear to ear. A construction worker with astonishing biceps.

When the children come home from school, sit and talk a few minutes.

Eat slowly, enjoying the food and the company.

If you're making a new picnic table, don't agonize to get finished. Enjoy making each saw cut perfect, each joint precise, each coat of varnish smooth.

Instead of thinking ahead to the hundred other things you've got to do or want to do, make up your mind to enjoy what you're doing now — whether it's mixing batter for a cake or writing a term paper or bathing the dog or clipping the bushes.

Believe sincerely that *now* is the most important time of your life. It's too late for yesterday and too early for tomorrow. The only thing that's real is today.

Cure Hyperopia by Accepting Christ Now

Are you planning to take up religion after you graduate from college and get married and begin raising a family — but you think that right now your friends would laugh at you, and besides, it would mean giving up some of the extracurricular activities you are now engaging in?

Are you planning someday to become a Christian, but postponing it because Christianity doesn't square very well with the way you are conducting your business?

Are you hoping to get back to church again soon, to learn about God and your relationship to Him, and to get back in contact with spiritual things — but right now you are just too busy, and Sunday is your only day to sleep late, and there just doesn't seem to be any other time to get that shopping and golfing out of the way, and maybe you'll have more time when you retire?

If so, you are suffering from spiritual hyperopia. In your farsightedness you can see the distant goal, but you cannot perceive the present responsibility in reaching that goal.

It's a most dangerous malady.

The number of people who receive salvation in their old age is infinitesimally small. It does happen, of course, for with God all things are possible. But it's highly unlikely.

It is said that Ty Cobb, probably the most talented and most hated baseball player who ever lived, received Christ on his deathbed. At that time he was reported to have said, "I'm just sorry I didn't do this during the first half of the first inning instead of the last half of the ninth."

In great wisdom the Bible says, "Remember also your Creator in the days of your youth, before the evil days come, and the years draw nigh, when you will say, 'I have no pleasure in them'" (Ecclesiastes 12:1).

You can get calluses on your heart just as you get calluses on your hands. Each time you say No to Christ you become more insensitive to Him. To be farsighted and say "I'll do it in the future" is not being very realistic.

Besides, the tomorrow you are counting on so heavily may never arrive.

Christ may arrive first. And "as the lightning comes from the east and flashes to the west, so will be the coming of the Son of Man" (Matthew 24:27). That doesn't leave much time for repentance.

Or, you may die first. Every day thousands of people die instantaneously in their automobiles, in their bathtubs, in their beds, and on golf courses. That doesn't leave much time for repentance, either.

Then, too, don't you think it's a bit insincere to tell God, "Later"? Isn't it an insult to His love and His intelligence to say, "When I've got time for You," or "After I've had my fun"? The Bible says, "Do not be deceived: God cannot be mocked. A man reaps what he sows" (Galatians 6:7).

51

"I tell you, now is the time of God's favor, now is the day of salvation" (2 Corinthians 6:2).

Combat Hyperopia by Developing the Ability to Change Focus

The cure for farsightedness is not nearsightedness.

Rather, the cure for both farsightedness and nearsightedness is *the ability to change focus when necessary.*

Ideal eyesight catches a glimpse of the great principle, then can change focus to see the immediate application of that principle.

Good eyesight is the ability to see the far-ahead goal, then can look down to see the first step which must be taken toward that goal.

The person who sees clearly can catch a vision of the ideal, then see equally clearly how that ideal can be accomplished.

He does not take up his hammer and saw without first consulting the blueprints; but neither does he consult the blueprints without taking up his hammer and saw.

He does not get behind the wheel without first looking at the map; but neither does he consult the map without getting behind the wheel.

He does not act without consulting God's Word; but neither does he consult the Word without acting accordingly.

He does not proceed without planning; but neither does he plan without proceeding.

In short, the person with good vision has the ability to change focus when necessary.

Eye Exercises

To Help Stamp Out Farsightedness

1. Divide a sheet of paper into three columns.
   a) In the left column list five goals you wish to ac-

complish within the next ten years. They may be in many areas — money, hobbies, education, work, family, love, religion, and service.

b) In the middle column, across from each goal, list what you have already done to accomplish that goal.

c) In the right column list what you are going to do today (not next year or next month or tomorrow, but *today*) to accomplish each of those goals.

d) Do it.

2. During the next five days read the letter of James, one chapter a day. Take note of all the practical advice it gives for bringing great ideals down to present action.

3. Smile at the mailman and the checkout girl, be courteous to the man at the service station, and be kind to the neighbor's dog.

4. If you still have children at home, take the time to sit and talk with them for an hour or two.

5. Secure the constitution of your club, your committee, your board, or your organization. Read it over carefully, taking special note of the goals listed there. Ask yourself, "Are we reaching these goals?" If not, bring the matter before the group, and begin laying some definite plans to do something about it.

6. Next time you have an errand to do, walk instead of drive, if possible. Open your eyes to see and enjoy everything along the way.

Eye Drops

For the Treatment of Farsightedness

1. "A man of understanding sets his face toward wisdom, but the eyes of a fool are on the ends of the earth."

Proverbs 17:24

2. "Do you not say, 'Four months more and then the harvest'? I tell you, open your eyes and look at the fields! They are ripe for harvest."

John 4:35

3. "Now is the time of God's favor, now is the day of salvation."

2 Corinthians 6:2

4. "What good is it, my brothers, if a man claims to have faith but has no deeds? Can such faith save him?"

James 2:14

Chapter 5

Getting Used to
the Dark

Have you ever gone into one of those restaurants which was so dark that you thought the electric company had shut off their electricity because they hadn't paid their bill?

All you can see, as you come in from the brightly lighted street, is a small sea of flickering candles and a dark form that comes to you and asks, "How many in your party, please?"

As the hostess marches onward, you feel your way hesitantly, bumping against well-padded leather seats and saying "Excuse me" to a table.

When finally you are seated, you can see the people in the next booth and even at the tables across the room. The waitresses' short skirts begin to take on a red hue, and the mural of a bullfighter on the wall becomes visible.

It becomes, in fact, light enough to see the menu, and then you know it can't be because of nonpayment of bills that the lights had been turned low. For some reason, the darker a restaurant is, the more expensive it is.

By the time you have your salad you can see the small "Rest Rooms" sign on the other side of the dining room, and when you receive your entrée the room is almost as bright as McDonald's.

The Eyes Adjust

You know, of course, that the restaurant isn't getting brighter. Rather, your eyes are adjusting to the darkness.

Two things happen within your eyes as you become used to the dark.

First of all, your pupils gradually become larger, allowing more light to enter your eyes.

Secondly, a chemical change takes place in the retina. (The retina is the back wall of the eye that changes light impulses into nerve impulses and then sends them to the brain by way of the optic nerve.) Though a great deal of light is falling on the retina, the chemical process is slowed, reducing the sensitivity of the retina to light. When the amount of light is diminished, a reverse chemical change takes place, again sensitizing the photo cells of the retina. This process takes more time than the simple opening and closing of the pupil, which explains why many minutes must elapse before a person can see well in the dark.

When you have finished your dessert, paid your bill, and stepped into the street, you are almost blinded by the bright light. You have to partially close your eyes and wait for the two processes to reverse themselves.

When you move quickly from a light place to a dark place, the change your eyes must make is quite dramatic. You are acutely aware of it, especially if you stumble over the furniture. But if the change is gradual, you may not even be aware of the creeping shadows of darkness.

You may, for instance, be sitting on a lounge chair in the backyard, reading the evening paper after dinner. Your daughter comes out of the house and says, "It's pitch black out here! How can you see well enough to read?" Only then are you aware that the last fingers of light are withdrawing from the western horizon, and it is indeed almost dark. Your eyes have adjusted so smoothly and perfectly to the darkness that you were not aware of the subtle withdrawal of light. You got used to the dark without realizing it.

Getting Used to the Dark Can Be Dangerous

This is a marvelous process, and it enables us to adjust more easily to a wide range of living conditions.

But it can also work against us.

I once read a childhood story of two small boys who were playing in a large, dense woods. Their mother knew there was a well-outlined path, and she had given them permission to stay there until just before the sun went down. She warned them sternly to leave the woods while it was still light so they could easily find their way home on the path. But they were having so much fun that they didn't notice the setting sun. Their eyes adjusted so gradually to the twilight that they weren't aware of the deepening gloom. Suddenly they became aware of the darkness. The path was no longer visible. As they began to try to find their way home they stumbled over roots, ran into trees, and became entangled in vines. I don't remember how the story ended, but it made a point with my youthful mind: When Mom tells you to come home before dark, you had better do it.

May we draw an analogy to the spiritual life?

Is it possible that the world is gradually desensitizing us to evil? Little by little is sin being made to appear less sinful? Could it be that the darkness is closing in so gradually, it doesn't even seem like darkness? Might it be that we, like these two boys, are getting used to the dark?

Item

Remember when *Playboy* was the most daring magazine on the market? Its "nudes," all of them artfully partially covered, were the talk of the town. They were sold under the counter, and businessmen sneaked them into their homes via briefcase.

Then "nudist" magazines appeared on the scene, discreetly filmed in nudist camps and touched up with an airbrush. Then somebody forgot how to use an airbrush.

Playboy retaliated by showing full frontal nudity. But the hard-core people began to publish intercourse pictures — first fake, then real. And *Playboy*, which hasn't gone all the way, has developed a case of poor circulation.

Thus far, access to pornographic bookstores is limited to persons eighteen or over. In view of the ability of the

American people to get used to the dark, how long do you suppose that law will be enforced?

Item

Most countries around the world are busy changing their abortion laws. They are at various stages along the way, but the usual pattern has been this: (1) all abortion illegal; (2) abortion legal if three doctors determine that the pregnancy endangers the physical life of the mother; (3) abortion legal if one doctor determines that the pregnancy endangers the physical or mental health of the mother; (4) abortion legal by consent of the mother for any reason, provided it is performed within ninety days of conception; (5) abortion on demand, at any time during pregnancy; (6) refusal to perform an abortion illegal.

Item

In 1969 a Gallup poll revealed that 68 percent of the American people believed premarital sex is wrong. In 1973 the figure was 48 percent.

Item

Euthanasia bills presented to state legislatures two and three years ago advocated "passive euthanasia," allowing a dying patient to die without attempting to prolong his life by extraordinary means. Bills being presented now are often "active euthanasia" bills, calling for speeding the death of a terminally ill patient by active means.

Item

Ten years ago the clinical textbooks listed homosexuality under "perversions."

More recently it was listed under "deviations."

In this year's copy of some major textbooks, homosexuality is categorized under "variations."

Item

Five years ago, newspaper editors were berating the nation's economists because the annual inflation rate was 3.2 percent. Now they write editorials rejoicing that the inflation rate is "only" 7 percent.

Item

Twenty-five years ago the elders in many American

churches were deeply concerned about declining attendance at the evening service. Ten years ago the elders were concerned about attendance at the morning service. Now the ministers are concerned about the elders' declining attendance at the morning service.

Item

When first released, the film *Midnight Cowboy* was rated "R." When re-released a few years later it was rated "PG."

Question

How can it be that Martha Mundane, fifty-nine-year-old maiden lady Sunday school teacher, is indicted for embezzling $450,000 from the bank that employed her?

Because eight years ago she took a few hundred dollars to pay medical bills, intending to repay it.

Question

Why is Arnold Fosdick dying of lung cancer?

Because at the age of fourteen he started smoking three cigarettes a day.

Question

Why is Madeline Mayor unable to prepare a decent meal for her family?

Because a year ago she began to drink a few cocktails with her soap operas to help her get through a boring day.

Question

Why are college students who go home for vacation shocked to discover how much gossiping their parents do?

Because when they lived at home they got so used to it they considered it normal.

Question

Why does John Happersmith use profanity in every sentence without being aware of it?

Because he began deliberately to use such words in grade school, to show off.

He's a Wily Old Devil

A typical religious cartoon pictures a teenager being invited to join a gang of boys on a drinking party. Satan

59

hovers near, complete with pitchfork, forked tail, and red underwear, whispering "Go ahead" in his ear.

Our young hero can say Yes or No, and that's that. It seems as if it ought to be such an easy, clear-cut decision. On one side are all the dirty, slimy, long-haired, drinking, cussing rowdies; and on the other side are the angels, God, Jesus, Goodness, Purity, and all the rest.

What the cartoonist has failed to mention is the spadework Satan has been doing for weeks, months, and years. The liquor ads. The six-packs in Dad's refrigerator. The good times the rowdies have. The boredom at the church youth meeting. That good-looking redhead. The student council election. The Gallup polls. His friends.

Maybe it ought to look like a choice between black and white. But the Deceiver has so polluted the air that our hero sees only shades of gray. The white no longer looks so white, and the black no longer looks so black.

Satan is called "the Prince of Darkness." But he knows better than to pull all the shades down at once. He uses the twilight technique; he pulls them down slowly enough to give our moral eyes time to compensate for the increasing gloom.

A Lesson From Biology

It takes nine months for a baby to grow in its hidden, quiet place before it emerges suddenly into the world, complete in all respects from fingerprints to blue eyes to gall bladder. A child's life does not really begin at birth. It begins at conception.

Not surprisingly, the word *conception* is used in connection with sin. Says James, "Each one is tempted when, by his own evil desire, he is dragged away and enticed. Then, after desire has conceived, it gives birth to sin; and sin, when it is full-grown, gives birth to death" (James 1:14, 15). When sin is born it emerges complete in all respects, but its conception has occurred long before. Between conception and birth there has been a time of quiet, slow, almost-unnoticed development.

The Book of Job uses a similar figure of speech to describe the godless: "They conceive mischief and bring forth evil and their heart prepares deceit" (Job 15:35).

Likewise Isaiah describes those who "conceive mischief and bring forth iniquity" (Isaiah 59:4), and David says, "Behold, the wicked man conceives evil, and is pregnant with mischief, and brings forth lies" (Psalm 7:14).

A Lesson From History

Abraham's nephew Lot didn't move immediately into the wicked city of Sodom. First he chose for himself the Jordan valley. Then he "dwelt among the cities of the valley and moved his tent as far as Sodom" (Genesis 13:12).

I doubt if Lot moved his tents cross-country in a moving van. More likely he moved them a few hundred feet at a time: first the countryside near Sodom, then the outskirts, then the suburbs, then into the heart of the city itself.

He had time to get used to the dark.

Avoid Getting Used to the Dark by Exposing Yourself to the Light

How do we avoid the dangers of getting used to the dark?

Remember, when you left that darkened restaurant, how the light shocked your eyes when you emerged into the street?

That's what it takes — a shocking beam of light.

John Happersmith, the curser, might be shocked if he heard himself on tape.

Arnold Fosdick received his beam of light when the doctor told him he had a spot on his lung. Unfortunately it was too late.

Perhaps Madeline Mayor will come to her senses, admit she has a problem, and seek help from A.A. Hopefully she will do this before the light comes in the form of a crunching automobile accident or the breakup of her marriage.

The hometown gossipers need somehow to be made aware of the perversity of their favorite pastime.

What we all need is more light.

That's exactly what Christ came to bring.

"I am the light of the world," He said. "Whoever follows me will never walk in darkness, but will have the light of life" (John 8:12).

"I have come into the world as a light, so that no one who believes in me should stay in darkness" (John 12:46).

Wherever He went, Jesus uncovered darkness for what it was. He did so, not by cursing the darkness, but by bringing light. He does the same today.

Let us take our actions and expose them to the light of Christ's life.

Let us take our thoughts and expose them to the light of His all-knowing intelligence.

Let us take our words and expose them to the light of His Word.

Let us take our attitudes and expose them to the light of His love.

Our standards ought not be determined by our society or our friends or our own sense of values or our parents. Out standard ought to be the one made visible by Jesus Christ, the Light of the World.

Avoid Getting Used to the Dark
by Becoming a Source of Light

"You are the light of the world. A city on a hill cannot be hidden. Neither do people light a lamp and put it under a bowl. Instead they put it on its stand, and it gives light to everyone in the house. In the same way, let your light shine before men, that they may see your good deeds and praise your Father in heaven" (Matthew 5:14-16).

We are to be distinctive, unique, different.

We are to light the world, not adjust to its darkness.

We are to light a candle, not curse the darkness.

We are to march ahead, showing the way; not march behind, stumbling in the ruts of others.

The deeper the darkness grows around us, the more distinctly our light will seem to shine. Have you ever noticed that when the lights are first turned on at a night football game, they appear not to be very bright against the twilight sky? As the darkness deepens, the lights seem to increase in intensity until they literally blaze in the sky.

We are to be this kind of light, blazing the more brightly as the gloom around us deepens. "Therefore do not be partners with them. For you were once darkness, but now you are light in the Lord. Live as children of light" (Ephesians 5:7,8).

In the company of profanity, the clean-tongued person will be distinctive.

In the presence of drunken revelry, sobriety will shine brightly.

Over the lunch boxes of racial slander, empathy will be a beam from a bright flashlight.

Over the dinner table of discontented grumbling, contented optimism will dance like a candle.

In the smoky rooms of political payoffs, honesty will stream like light from an open window.

In the murk of crib notes and purchased answers, an honest exam will glow with quiet dignity.

Amid the smut of newsstands and magazine racks, our Bible and Christian literature will be bright witnesses to our faith.

Eye Exercises

1. Find in a newspaper or magazine an "Item" to add to the list in this chapter — an illustration of how society's standards are gradually changing. (Remember, of course, that not all changes are for the worse.)

2. How is the ethical climate of your generation different from that of your parents? How is it different from

that of your children? How is the change for the better, for the worse, or mixed?

3. Examine yourself. Have your personal standards changed during the last six months? The last two years? The last ten years?

Are you getting more broad-minded? Or is your conscience stretching?

4. Is there a standard that remains constant in changing times? Are some of the biblical precepts meant for that time only, while others are meant for all times? If so, how do you determine which is which?

5. Determine that tomorrow at work you will be distinctive in some particular way — not just to draw attention to yourself, but to be a light in a murky environment.

Eye Drops

*To Prevent You From Adjusting
to the Darkness*

1. "After desire has conceived, it gives birth to sin; and sin, when it is full-grown, gives birth to death."

James 1:15

2. "Abram dwelt in the land of Canaan, while Lot dwelt among the cities of the valley and moved his tent as far as Sodom."

Genesis 13:12

3. "I am the light of the world. Whoever follows me will never walk in darkness, but will have the light of life."

John 8:12

4. "You are the light of the world."

Matthew 5:14a

Chapter 6

Foreign Objects in the Eye

The human eye is at the same time one of the most delicate and most important parts of the body. Because of this, God has gone to extraordinary measures to protect your eyes from injury by foreign objects.

God has provided a place for the eyes inside the skull instead of outside it. They are protected by the bony protrusions of a brow above, cheekbones below, and the bridge of the nose between.

God has installed tear ducts that constantly bathe your eyes. When a speck of foreign matter enters the eye cavity, floods of clear fluid are there to wash it away.

He has hedged them above with eyebrows, to reroute the runoff of sweat from the brow.

He has equipped them with eyelashes that extend out over the eyes, both above and below, to catch objects blowing in the wind.

He has provided shutters that not only close to give them protection during sleep, but are equipped with lightning-quick reflex devices that snap the eyes shut automatically when danger comes near.

And He has given you two eyes instead of one. (He could, you know, have given you two noses and one eye.)

Despite all these truly remarkable protection devices, foreign objects still manage to get into the eyes from time to time.

The wind can carry flying specks of sand, dust, and ashes into the eyes. Smog hanging heavy in the air will irritate the eyes. Pollen can irritate both the eyes and their owners. Then there are those dangerous missiles such as pellets, pins, needles, and paper airplanes.

The Most Dangerous Foreign Object

There is one foreign object, however, for which the body seems to have no natural protection.

That foreign object can cause more harm than almost any other, because it affects not only the eye but the entire personality.

That foreign object is a *plank*.

Jesus, the Great Physician and the world's greatest authority on eyes, said this about it:

> Why do you look at the speck of sawdust in your brother's eye and pay no attention to the plank in your own eye? How can you say to your brother, "Let me take the speck out of your eye," when all the time there is a plank in your own eye? You hypocrite, first take the plank out of your own eye, and then you will see clearly to remove the speck from your brother's eye.
>
> *Matthew 7:3-5*

And there are some who picture Jesus as always the earnest, somber, solemn one? Here He exhibits a beautiful sense of humor!

He drives home a powerful point with a sketch that is so absurd it is comical: a man telling a friend to hold still while he removes that bit of dust from his eye — while at the same time a huge, bloody plank protrudes from his own eye!

Is it possible that someone could be that stupid? With the eyes of the body, perhaps not. With the eyes of the mind, yes. Fallen human nature is capable of many strange quirks. This is one of them that Jesus, the Divine Opthalmologist, came to cure.

Two Problems in One

This particular kind of defective vision creates not really one problem, but two.

The first problem is that *we tend to be keenly aware of the faults of others while oblivious to our own.* It's easier to see the foreign object in another's eye than it is to see it in our own.

The second problem is that *we tend to confuse the less important with the more important.* We think sawdust specks are as large as planks, and planks as small as sawdust specks.

These two traits of bad vision occur simultaneously. The eyes play two tricks at once. By some incredible process of self-deception we see the other's speck and miss our own plank.

We are ready to reform somebody else, because his fault looms large in our mind's eye; but we are not ready to reform ourselves, simply because we don't see the necessity for it.

Some Commonplace Specks and Planks

Now let's bring Jesus' observation up to date. Let's take His question, "Why do you look at the speck of sawdust in your brother's eye and pay no attention to the plank in your own eye?" and translate it into our everyday situations. For instance:

Why do you criticize your church for being "dead" while at the same time you stir up trouble?

Why do you complain about being lonesome, when you have made no effort to visit anybody?

Father, why do you criticize your son for experimenting with cigarettes, while you, an adult, helplessly puff away on two packs a day?

Mother, why do you nag your daughter about the way she combs her hair, while you constantly bicker with your husband?

Why do you criticize Mrs. Andrews for her red wig, though you have a wonderful singing voice you aren't using?

Why do you complain about the eight-cent increase in

the price of a can of beans, while you spend $6.95 each to eat at a fancy restaurant?

Why do you complain about a fellow employee who is always buttering up the boss, while you don't even get your work done?

Why are you embarrassed by your father's funny stories, though yours are dirty stories?

Why are you embarrassed by your mother's accent, when your speech is punctuated by foul words?

Why do you condemn minority groups for public disorder, while you are disobeying the United States Constitution which promises life, liberty, and the pursuit of happiness to all citizens?

Why do you criticize the younger generation for experimenting with drugs while at the same time you need a pill to get to sleep, three cups of coffee to wake up, a cocktail to lubricate your tongue at a party, pills to help you diet, and tranquilizers to help you cope with a visit by the in-laws?

Why do you say, "I don't see why our church always does it this way," while at the same time saying, "I couldn't possibly help"?

Why do you criticize another's long prayer in a public meeting, while you are afraid to say even a sentence prayer?

The possibilities are endless, and you may wish to write some of your own (see "Eye Exercises" at the end of this chapter).

More Specks and Planks

Let's take another look at the difference between sawdust specks and planks. What kind of contrast do you suppose Jesus was trying to draw?

Perhaps He was talking about —

— specks of manners and planks of morals.
— specks of ritual and planks of religion.
— specks of style and planks of content.
— specks of thoughtlessness and planks of hatred.

— specks of pettiness and planks of pride.

In other words, let's get our sense of values straight; let's not place major emphasis on minor matters and vice versa.

The Biggest Plank of All

We must not miss one very important point — namely, that *the critical attitude itself is often the plank in our own eye.*

This was the case with the Pharisee who happened to be praying in the temple at the same time as the publican. Just in case God hadn't noticed, he took pains to point out all the specks he saw in the publican's eye — robbery, adultery, and so forth. Then he pointed out (again, just in case the Almighty hadn't noticed) the marvelous spiritual eyesight that he himself had: "I fast twice a week and give a tenth of all my income" (Luke 18:12). Yet the Pharisee had a plank sticking right through his eye, a plank he was completely unaware of. No, it wasn't a plank of robbery, adultery, or covetousness. It was the plank of *spiritual pride.* It was a plank of heavenly snobbishness, of conceit, of a critical attitude toward others.

What is the plank in the eye of the housewife who sits by the phone spreading the story about Billy Anderson's arrest for drunken driving? Is it not *sitting by the phone?*

What is the plank in the eye of Mrs. Jones, running from woman to woman complaining about the way the Ladies' League is being run? Is it not *running* and *complaining?*

What is the plank in the eye of Evangelist Smith who publicly criticizes the methods of Evangelist Brown? Is it not the *public criticism?*

What is the plank in the eye of the Bible College professor who condemns every other view except that of his own college? Is it not the *attitude of condemnation?*

What about the church member who is continually sleuthing for heresy from the pulpit? Is it not the *sleuthing* itself that is the plank in his eye?

The judgmental attitude is the greatest plank of all. That's why Jesus made sure no one misunderstood what He was saying: "Do not judge, or you too will be judged" (Matthew 7:1).

Never Make Judgments?

"Does this mean," you ask, "that I should never make judgments about people?"

No. It can't possibly mean that. Jesus instructed His followers to do things like stamping their feet in the dust of the villages that did not receive them, not casting their pearls before swine, and avoiding the leaven of the Pharisees. None of these can be done without making some kind of judgment.

We are constantly called upon to make judgments about other people's character, personality, and ability. In hiring, firing, choosing friends, dating, disciplining children, settling disputes, arriving at verdicts in courts of law, and in hundreds of other situations, such decisions are both legitimate and necessary.

Jesus is talking, not about making judgments, but about *being judgmental*. There is a difference.

Being judgmental is gloating over the evil that has been uncovered. It is hoping to find the bad, then feeling self-righteous about the whole thing.

Being judgmental is looking at specks with a magnifying glass. It is making public announcements about the faults of others.

Being judgmental is jumping to conclusions — the worst ones. It is being a jury that automatically finds the defendant guilty as charged before hearing the case. It is presuming to know the whole story before hearing the whole story.

Judgmental Attitudes Come Full Circle

"For in the same way you judge others, you will be judged, and with the measure you use, it will be measured to you" (Matthew 7:2).

A man in one of the author's former congregations was always critical of persons with emotional and mental problems. "If they walked right with the Lord," he would say, "they wouldn't have problems like that." Then his wife, a fine Christian woman, had a mental breakdown, and for two years he had to visit her in an institution. It was a hard pill to swallow.

Somehow we will always reap what we sow. If we are kind in our assessments of others, they will be kind in their assessments of us. If we are critical of them, we can expect them to be critical of us.

I may not be able to see the log in my own eye, but it is obvious to everyone else. When I self-righteously offer to help remove the speck in someone else's eye, I can rightfully expect them to snicker in my face.

What to Do About Planks and Specks

1. *Genuinely pray for someone you are tempted to criticize.*

You will notice the emphasis on *genuine* prayer. The prayer of the Pharisee was a parade of pride, not really a prayer at all. We've all heard prayers that went something like this: "Lord, we thank Thee that we have answered the call to serve You, and we pray that other members of the church may be more conscientious and dedicated."

It's really quite difficult to kneel in a genuine prayer for pregnant school-dropout Anne Jones — and then get on the telephone to tell your neighbors that it didn't surprise you at all because you always knew she was wild, just as her mother used to be.

2. *Love those whom you are tempted to criticize.*

Christian love is more than a feeling of attraction. It doesn't always mean approval. "While we were still sinners, Christ died for us" (Romans 5:8).

Christian love is a deliberate act of the will to be concerned for another's welfare. It seeks the best for the other person.

Is your neighbor a cranky old lady? Then love her. Bake her a cake. Offer to take her to the store. Demonstrate to her and tell her that God loves her.

Is your son's teacher a poor disciplinarian? Love her — not because of what she is, but in spite of it. Pledge your cooperation. Encourage her to be strong.

3. *Try to walk in the other person's shoes.*

There are always reasons why people are the way they are. The reasons may not always justify their behavior, but at least they help to explain it.

Take Mr. Smith, down the street. He dislikes children. If a child so much as skips off the sidewalk and steps onto his lawn, he bursts out the front door like a bull. And if the Eighth Street baseball gang should hit a foul ball under his bushes, it's good-by forever.

But there must be reasons for his anti-childrenism. Perhaps he was once beaten by a gang of junior-high boys. Maybe his wife was run down by a bicycle, breaking her hip and making her an invalid. Perhaps he is bitter because he has no grandchildren of his own. Is it possible that he has hardening of the arteries, which impairs his ability to think clearly? His reaction to children might even go back to a disturbing experience of his own childhood, when he was rejected by his playmates. Whatever the reason, the point is: There is a reason.

Let us apply this kind of thinking to someone we are tempted to be judgmental of.

4. *Examine your own motives.*

Just as there are reasons why others act the way they do, so there are reasons why we act the way we do. If we are critical and judgmental, we can be sure there is a reason.

It might be educational to discover what those reasons are.

Your reason, for instance, for criticizing how much Georgia Ozzeldorp spends on clothes — might it be that you wish you had that much to spend?

And your reason for blazing out so strongly against

those convicted or suspected of sexual sins — might it lie somewhere in your own frustrations?

Your criticism of the way John Doakes is handling the cashier's job at the bank — could it have something to do with the fact that you wanted the job?

Your comments about Reverend Blow's sheep-stealing habits — might you not speak differently if it hadn't been your sheep that were stolen?

Specks, you see, are very small. Usually you don't notice a bit of dust floating around in someone's eye socket. But if you have an ulterior motive for looking for one, you're likely to find it.

5. *Clear up your own faults first.*

"You hypocrite, first take the plank out of your own eye, and then you will see clearly to remove the speck from your brother's eye" (Matthew 7:5).

It is our own faults, you see, which make it impossible to evaluate properly the conduct of others. Till we can see clearly we will not judge fairly.

This is why God alone is the only fair judge. His decisions are not colored by faulty ethics, nor His judgments distorted by greed, envy, or prejudice.

"But," you say, "that means I can never qualify, because I will never be perfect in this life."

That's right. You got the point.

Eye Exercises

For the Distorted Vision That Sees
Specks and Misses Planks

1. Write a number of your own versions of Jesus' statement "Why do you look at the speck of sawdust in your brother's eye and pay no attention to the plank in your own eye?" The author has provided several of these in the section, "Some Commonplace Specks and Planks," but he's certain you have some original ones to add to the list.

2. Review the five points under "What to Do About

Planks and Specks," this time personalizing each one.

For point 1, you might do this: On a piece of paper write the heading, "Genuinely pray for someone you are tempted to criticize." List the names of two or three people whom you have criticized lately. Then pray for each one individually, mentioning specific needs.

Follow a similar pattern for each of the other points. For number 4, for example, write "Examine your own motives." Below it list the matters that you are most critical about. Then try to figure out *why* those particular things aggravate you so much.

Eye Drops

To Wash Planks From Eyes

1. "Do not judge, or you too will be judged."

Matthew 7:1

2. "Why do you look at the speck of sawdust in your brother's eye and pay no attention to the plank in your own eye?"

Matthew 7:3

3. "Love does not delight in evil but rejoices in the truth."

1 Corinthians 13:6

4. "Brothers, if a man is trapped in some sin, you who are spiritual should restore him gently. But watch yourself; you also may be tempted."

Galatians 6:1

Chapter 7
Color Blindness
(a) Black-sightedness
The Color Blindness That Sees Only the Bad

What Color Blindness Is

Color blindness is the inability to distinguish colors properly. For the color-blind person, the various shades of color are muddled and distorted. He may, in fact, not be able to distinguish certain colors from one another, such as red and green.

Color blindness is a remarkably sexist malady. One in every ten males is afflicted with it, but it affects only one of every two hundred females. It is caused by a hereditary deficiency in the chromosomes that determine sex.

Some species of the animal world are almost entirely color-blind. The world of dogs and cats, for instance, is a world of light, dark, and grays. Others have color perception far better than ours. Most monkeys, squirrels, and birds have far better color vision than humans, probably because it is essential in their search for food.

A story is told about the first researcher who studied color blindness scientifically, the nineteenth-century English chemist John Dalton. Mr. Dalton was himself color-blind. He was also a devout Quaker, and he showed up one day at a prayer meeting wearing a pair of bright red stockings that a practical joker had switched for his somber gray ones.

The handicap of color deficiency can eliminate many people from the vocations of their choice. Our modern world is highly color-oriented, and the ability to accurately distinguish colors is necessary in such fields as cosmetics, photography, aviation, textiles, railroading, electronics, decoration, telephone repair, and many others. Red and green, the most commonly confused colors, were unfortunately chosen for signal lights.

There is another kind of color deficiency, however, which is even more serious. That deficiency is the tendency to see things in terms of one color only.

We are talking, of course, not about the physical eyes, but about the mental, psychological, and spiritual eyes. We are talking about attitudes that a person brings to bear upon everything he sees. We are talking about the kind of judgments he immediately tends to make.

In these chapters we will discuss three important kinds of color blindness: black-sightedness, rose-sightedness, and green-sightedness. There are more types, to be sure, but these are rather common and serious ones.

Some Symptoms of Black-sightedness

If someone says to you, "It certainly is nice today, isn't it?" do you reply, "Yes, but stormy weather is predicted for tomorrow"?

When your husband brings home a bouquet of flowers, do you wonder what sin he's trying to atone for?

When your wife gives you an extra warm embrace, do you try to decide whether it's a new coat or a new dishwasher she's working on?

If you see a neighbor riding down the street with a man who is not her husband, do you figure she's stepping out on her husband?

As you stand at the check-out counter of the supermarket, do you think to yourself that the cash register is programmed to add an extra fifty cents to your bill without even pressing the keys?

When your hostess passes the mashed potatoes for the third time, do you think to yourself, "She's trying to get me to gain weight so I won't look as good as she does"?

When you leave the room at a party, do you wonder what they're saying about you when you're gone?

When your daughter leaves with a date, are you just sure they are headed straight for a motel?

When your boss compliments you on your work, do you begin to wonder what unsavory job he's about to transfer you to?

Perhaps you catch yourself saying things like —

"It won't work anyway."

"It may be a good idea, but you'll never get people to cooperate."

"It may be a good idea, but we're not ready for it yet."

"It may have been a good idea last year, but it's too late now."

"I suspected it all the time."

If so, you probably have black-sightedness.

A Common Ailment

As a physical ailment, this type of color blindness is very rare.

As an ailment of the attitude, it is quite common.

Black-sightedness is seeing blackness everywhere, in the sense that black is symbolic of evil. It is viewing everyone, everything, and every situation with suspicion. It is seeing evil lurking in every corner even when there is little or no evidence for it.

I once read of a man who tried to give away $100 in dollar bills on the streets of New York. After an entire day of trying he still had $17 left. People just wouldn't accept them. Mugging, robbery, and pickpocketing they could believe. Free dollar bills, with no strings attached, they could not believe. They saw black.

The House Judiciary Committee spent week after week questioning Nelson Rockefeller about the gifts he had given to acquaintances and friends. He had laid out sums like $18,000, $25,000, and $50,000. They explored, sleuthed, and cross-examined in an attempt to find out what his ulterior motives were. What did he hope to gain politically? What did he hope to gain financially? They finally gave up. It was hopeless. Apparently the only reason Mr. Rockefeller gave away money was because somebody needed it and he thought the recipient was worthy. This simply boggled the minds of the good senators. Graft, payoffs, kickbacks, influence-buying, bribery — all these they could understand. But generosity without expectation of return — this they could not comprehend.

The late C. S. Lewis in his classic, *The Screwtape Letters*, gives us a thoughtful insight into the nature of the Evil One. Satan, he says, cannot understand the love of God or the love humans have for one another. His eyesight is so blackened by his own hatred that he cannot comprehend the concept of love. The nerve endings of his retina are not sensitive to goodness; they respond only to black.

I once worked with a man who had his mind in the gutter at least 88 percent of his waking hours. He read the most sordid of meanings into the most innocent of remarks. In the eyes, the walk, and the talk of every female passerby he detected smoldering lust. A tree reminded him of a dirty story. An automobile reminded him of a dirty story. A flower reminded him of a dirty story. A baseball reminded him of a dirty story. And, of course, a dirty story reminded him of another dirty story.

He was a living testimony of the truth of Jesus' words, "If your eyes are bad, your whole body will be full of darkness. If then the light within you is darkness, how great is that darkness!" (Matthew 6:23).

But dark-sightedness is not limited to the leering, lascivious type. It can sometimes be a very real problem with the pious, clasped-hand, eyes-upward person. I have in my study a book on "worldly amusements," by an evangelist who was well known a few decades ago. In this short volume he evaluates a great number of amusements, sports, and games. He concludes that there is a mortal danger in almost everything except dominoes and checkers. Movies, of course, lead straight to hell. Dancing is one of the worst of all evils because of the physical movement and contact. Swimming is good exercise, but because of the danger of gazing at each other's half-naked bodies, participants should swim in sex-segregated areas. Circuses are questionable because of the skimpiness of the costumes of lady performers, as are football and basketball games where twirling, jumping, and somersaulting cheerleaders expose appalling portions of epidermis.

The good preacher expresses shock at the immorality of the day; but he might be even more shocked at the implications of the Scripture: "To the pure, all things are pure, but to those who are corrupted and do not believe, nothing is pure. In fact, both their minds and consciences are corrupted" (Titus 1:15).

Combat Black-sightedness
by Evaluating Yourself

It has been observed that most of our suspicions are aroused by what we know of ourselves. Shakespeare said, "Suspicion always haunts the guilty mind."

Could it be that you are suspicious of the check-out register because if you were the manager of the supermarket you would have it "adjusted"?

Could it be that some of the same senators who were so suspicious of Nelson Rockefeller were judging him by themselves?

Is it perhaps because you seldom give a compliment without an ulterior motive that you suspect others of the same?

Do you suspect your neighbor of stepping out because

that is what you would do if you had the opportunity?

Do your suspicions about your daughter have anything to do about your own dating habits?

Before we judge others too harshly, let us engage in some soul-searching to see whether we ourselves are guilty of the very things we suspect in others.

It's just possible that if we can see ourselves in a true light, we will look upon others more favorably.

Combat Black-sightedness
by Finding Out All the Facts

One of the chief causes of black-sightedness is ignorance. We tend to make harsh judgments simply because we don't know all the facts.

Have you ever put together a jigsaw puzzle and found out that there were a number of pieces missing? And how did the empty spots look? Dark. That's the way it often is when we try to fill in the missing details of a story: They appear black.

A little knowledge is a dangerous thing.

Combat Black-sightedness
by Rejoicing in the Good

One of the best treatments for black-sightedness is love. And one of the characteristics of love, according to 1 Corinthians 13:6, is that it "does not delight in evil but rejoices in the truth."

According to the New English Bible, "Love keeps no score of wrongs; does not gloat over other men's sins, but delights in the truth."

And, in the Phillips version we read, "It does not keep account of evil or gloat over the wickedness of other people. On the contrary, it is glad with all good men when truth prevails."

This description of love emphasizes that the person

who displays true Christian love wants the best to happen rather than the worst. He does not rub his hands in glee when he hears the latest sordid gossip. He does not specialize in bad news. He does not monopolize the conversation with stories of blood, gore, and gloom. He gets no satisfaction in finding out that a famous statesman is really a crook and that a well-known evangelist is a thief.

I once read of a famous baseball pitcher who listened to a young mother tell a moving story about how her daughter was dying of leukemia and how they desperately needed money for treatments. He wrote out a check for a thousand dollars. Later he found that the woman's story about her daughter was a hoax.

The baseball player's response was, "That's the best thing I've heard all year."

"You mean you're glad your money is wasted?" asked a startled friend.

"No," he replied, "I mean I'm happy that she doesn't really have a little girl who has leukemia."

That's rejoicing in the good.

Combat Black-sightedness
by Believing the Best

Another characteristic of love, according to 1 Corinthians 13:7, is that "it always protects, always trusts, always hopes, always perseveres."

The Living Bible translates it this way: "If you love someone you will be loyal to him no matter what the cost. You will always believe in him, always expect the best of him, and always stand your ground in defending him."

In summary, love is willing to believe the best about others. In making judgments it is more likely to be too gentle rather than too harsh. If there is a doubt, it gives the other fellow the benefit of the doubt.

Let us accept compliments graciously and be grateful for them, without questioning the giver's motives.

If the clerk makes an error, let us point it out. But let us try to assume that it was an honest error.

If she says you have a good-looking jacket, assume that she truly considers it a good-looking jacket.

If he comes home with flowers for the first time in three years, try to believe he is just a little slow in thinking of things like that.

Combat Black-sightedness by Concentrating on the Beautiful

"Finally, brothers," said Paul as he finished his letter to the church at Philippi, "whatever is true, whatever is noble, whatever is right, whatever is pure, whatever is lovely, whatever is admirable — if anything is excellent or praiseworthy — think about such things" (Philippians 4:8).

If you think about things with these characteristics, you can't think black. You will be thinking in terms of colors, brightness, and pleasantness.

A constant stimulation by sordid novels, sordid movies, and sordid conversation will affect your spiritual retina. It will incline you to see black.

But stimulation by that which is uplifting, inspirational, beautiful, funny, and thought-provoking will sensitize your spiritual retina to that which is bright and colorful.

There's a Sunday school song that goes like this: "Be careful, little eyes, what you see. . . . There's a Father up above looking down on us in love, so be careful, little eyes, what you see." The tune may be childish, but the message is definitely adult.

Examine the kinds of magazines you read and the types of television programs you watch. Do they tend toward the beautiful, or to the brackish?

Take note of the philosophy held by the authors of the stories and novels you read. Does it tend to sour your mind, or sweeten it?

Listen carefully to the conversation of your friends over the coffee table, outside church, and at the bowling alley. Does it encourage you to walk away thinking about the attractive, or about the ugly?

Does this mean that every novel, television program, or moving picture a person shares must be all sweetness and light? Of course not.

Some so-called "Christian" novels of years past (and a few of the present) are so saccharine-sweet, they cause the reader to gag. They are entirely unrealistic and untrue, with no resemblance to life as it really is. To insist only on this is to err on the other side, to have rose-sightedness (see the next chapter).

What is important is the *intent* of the author, the scriptwriter, or the producer. The old classic novel and film, *The Grapes of Wrath*, for instance, painted a vivid picture of the horrid plight of the migrant workers in America, complete with many unsavory details. Yet it filled every requirement of the above verse (i.e., true, noble, right, pure, lovely, and admirable) because it promoted the cause of truth, nobility, righteousness, purity, loveliness, and the admirable.

As vitamin A helps the eyes, so grade A reading and thinking material help the eyes.

As we carefully select the diet that comprises bodily food, let us carefully select the diet that comprises our mental and spiritual food.

Combat Black-sightedness by Seeking Professional Help, If Necessary

If you are constantly seeing black, and if you are always suspicious of others, it may indicate that you need professional psychiatric help.

If your black judgments of others seem to be compulsive and there is little you can do about them, it is probably best to get aid from someone else.

83

If your judgments of others are based largely on feelings rather than evidence, you may not be thinking rationally.

Ask a close friend or a loved one whether your suspicions seem to be based on facts or reasonable assumptions. If not, please do something about it.

Don't be ashamed. As more study is being made of emotional disorders, it is becoming apparent that many of them are caused by an imbalance of body chemistry. The cure is as much medical as it is mental. Such problems are no more to be ashamed of than a gall bladder operation. Do not hesitate. Mental pain can hurt more than physical pain. Why be miserable?

Eye Exercises

To Help Keep Out the Blackness

1. Check the contents of your magazine rack and your bookcase. What kind of diet do they provide for your mind?

2. Keep a record of the television programs you and the members of your family watch in a week's time. What percentage of them pass the test of Philippians 4:8? Ditto with movies.

3. When a shady story is told at a party, neglect to laugh.

4. Refrain from all gossip for an entire week.

5. Resolve to read at least one of the great classic novels by the end of the month.

6. You catch a glimpse of a fellow church member in a supermarket, over there by the pork and beans — a member with whom you have not been on the best terms. She looks right at you, then turns away without so much as a nod or a smile. What do you think you saw? A social snub? Or a preoccupied shopper who perhaps was wondering where to find the macaroni or was adding up her purchases in her head to see if $30 would pay for it?

What do you see when you observe (a) a teenager running through your backyard; (b) a minister preaching a stewardship sermon; and (c) a woman riding in the car with one of your community leaders?

Eye Drops

To Clear Up That Dark Cloudiness

1. "If your eyes are bad, your whole body will be full of darkness. If then the light within you is darkness, how great is that darkness!"

Matthew 6:23

2. "To the pure, all things are pure, but to those who are corrupted and do not believe, nothing is pure."

Titus 1:15

3. "Love does not delight in evil but rejoices in the truth."

1 Corinthians 13:6

4. "Finally, brothers, whatever is true, whatever is noble, whatever is right, whatever is pure, whatever is lovely, whatever is admirable — if anything is excellent or praiseworthy — think about such things."

Philippians 4:8

Chapter 8
Color Blindness
(b) Rose-sightedness
The Color Blindness That Sees Only the Good

Rose-sightedness is the inability to see black. The person who has this weakness is unable to detect adequately such things as evil, injustice, and general cussedness. Things look rosy when they really aren't.

Rose-sightedness is the failure to recognize badness under its own nose. "So when the woman saw that the tree was good for food, and that it was a delight to the eyes, and that the tree was to be desired to make one wise, she took of its fruit and ate" (Genesis 3:6).

It was the false prophets of Israel who said, "Peace, peace," when there was no peace (Jeremiah 6:14).

It was the true prophets of the Lord who said, "Woe to those who are at ease in Zion" (Amos 6:1), who saw the evil in the land and warned about the judgment of God. They did not have rose vision.

Rose-sightedness is a cheery kind of problem. The victim feels no discomfort — at least, until it's too late. He keeps on believing the best, even though the worst has been exposed. He takes incriminating evidence and discards it as irrelevant. Instead of being concerned and alarmed, he is nonchalant. Instead of being uptight, he hangs loose. Instead of weeping, he keeps on whistling.

Others may see the true color and try to tell him, but he will remain unconvinced. In fact, the more advanced the disease, the jollier the patient may become.

Sometimes color blindness is a cop-out, an excuse for not accepting one's responsibility. After all, if you don't believe a problem exists, why do anything about it?

There are a few people to whom everything looks rosy. In most cases, however, rose-sightedness is selective. It is limited to certain situations, certain people, and certain incidents. Let us note a few of the more common types to be alert for.

Avoid the Rose-sightedness That Allows Itself to Be Deceived

In a way, it's fine to be trusting. It's pleasant to have confidence in the honesty and integrity of people.

Unfortunately it's not always wise. Frankly, there are a lot of people around who have no honesty and no integrity.

Eve's problem was that she was too quick to believe what she was told: "You will not die. For God knows that when you eat of it your eyes will be opened, and you will be like God, knowing good and evil" (Genesis 3:4,5).

The well-dressed man at the door says he is a bank examiner. His bank suspects that one of its tellers is embezzling money, and would you be so kind as to help set a trap for this dishonest person? The plan is to withdraw $5,000 and place it in his trust, etc., etc. Do you think you'll ever see your $5,000 again? Of course not.

You are walking at the shopping mall, and a woman nearby lets out a little scream. You run over to her and find her opening an envelope that she says she just found lying on the ground beside the bench. She gasps as she counts it — $20,000 in bills. Since you were so kind as to come over, she says, she will share it with you, 50-50. But just to prove yourself, could you please put up about $3,000 as an indication of your good faith? If you do, will you ever see that $3,000 again? You've got rose-sightedness if you think you will.

Let's face it. Some people are dishonest. They may be well dressed, have pleasant faces, and even have blond hair, but their hearts are black.

Jesus said, "Do not give dogs what is sacred; do not throw your pearls to pigs. If you do, they may trample them under their feet, and then turn and tear you to pieces" (Matthew 7:6).

That's a fascinating verse with many implications that we cannot get into here. But essentially it means we should not be duped by those who want to use us in one way or another and then will turn against us. We must see them for what they are — "dogs" and "pigs."

This may seem harsh, but it comes from the mouth of Jesus — the same Jesus who called the Pharisees "hypocrites" and "whitewashed tombs" (Matthew 23:27).

Of Him we read, "But Jesus would not trust himself to them, for he knew all men. He did not need man's testimony about man, for he knew what was in a man" (John 2:24, 25).

Jesus certainly didn't have rose-sightedness. Perfection does not imply naïveté.

Jesus advocated love, but He also advocated due caution when dealing with other people. "I am sending you out like sheep among wolves," He said. "Therefore be as shrewd as snakes and as innocent as doves. But be on your guard against men" (Matthew 10:16, 17).

We are to love, but not to love stupidly.

We are to give, but not to give foolishly.

We are to be idealistic, but also to be realistic.

Avoid Rose-sightedness
When Choosing a Marriage Partner

Someone has said, "Keep your eyes wide open before marriage and half-closed afterward."

Once you're married, you have a responsibility to make it work with whomever you've got. But before you're married you have a great responsibility to determine whether you're getting the right one.

Yes, it may sometimes be necessary to keep your eyes half-closed afterward, but that's no excuse for not having them wide open beforehand.

One of the biggest problems of dating is rose-sightedness.

Take the case of Mary Williamson.

Mary is a rather quiet girl, never accused of being shockingly beautiful, a Christian believer from a strict Baptist background, active in the youth group at church and the art club at school, but definitely not the cheerleader type. She never had a real date until her senior year in high school. Then she meets Jeff. Jeff — with his red motorcycle, his jet-black eyes, confident walk, hearty laugh, and uninhibited and public displays of affection for her. There are a few disturbing things — the occasional smell of beer on his breath, his profanity when he didn't think she could hear, his three speeding violations, his refusal to have anything to do with church, his flirtations with other girls, and his disinterest in getting a job.

All these little things will pass, Mary is sure, after they get married. After all, hasn't he promised her that as soon as he says "I do" he will settle right down and become a model husband in every respect? Except, of course, for two nights out a week with the boys. Her parents tell her it won't work out, and her friends tell her it won't work out. But she believes that love conquers all and that this is the greatest opportunity of her life.

The truth is, it won't work out. If she stays with him, she'll spend the rest of her life trying to take care of three kids at home while her out-of-work overgrown-adolescent husband drinks and rides motorcycles with the "boys." Church? Forget it.

Poor Mary. Her only real fault is rose-sightedness. She is so sincere, and she tries so hard. But she can't see very well. And it will ruin much of her life.

Avoid Rose-sightedness
When Looking at Your Children

The mother of Lee Harvey Oswald said, "He was always such a good boy." She was looking through rose-colored lenses.

When you view your children, you don't want to be black-sighted, of course. You don't want to see them as Little Monsters — or Big Monsters, as the case may be.

But neither should you want to see them as Sweet Little Things — or Sweet Big Things, as the case may be.

Realistically speaking, they are a mixture of good and bad, sweet and sour, righteousness and wickedness.

As a Christian parent you have an obligation to bring them up "in the way of the Lord." This includes encouraging their goodness and discouraging their badness.

But how can you discourage their badness if you don't see any? How can you help them to overcome their weaknesses if you refuse to admit that they have any?

We'd like to have you take a little test to see how much rose-sightedness you have toward your children. Please consider carefully before marking the appropriate lines.

Situation 1. Your son's fourth grade teacher, Mrs. Hamilton, calls you in for a conference. She tells you that your little Johnny refuses to do his work, fools around constantly, bothers the other children, and talks back to the teacher. Your immediate reaction is:

a) — "Mrs. Hamilton is an inexperienced teacher who cannot handle discipline problems very well."

b) — "Johnny wouldn't do any of those nasty things."

c) — "Most boys of Johnny's age are too active to enjoy school, and hence they get restless."

d) — "Johnny is so intelligent that he is bored with school."

e) — "For some unknown reason Mrs. Hamilton has a grudge against Johnny."

f) — "It's probably true that Johnny refuses to do his work, fools around constantly, bothers the other children, and talks back to the teacher."

g) — "When I get home I will have a long talk with Johnny's father, and then together we will have a long talk with Johnny."

h) — "Mrs. Hamilton is to be commended for calling me in."

Situation 2. Your eighth grader, Becky, seems to have no real friends. She walks to the bus stop alone, stands there alone while the other girls are in clusters, and walks home alone. She seldom gets asked to slumber parties or any other kind of social function. She has one friend, Judy, whom she is with constantly at church and school. She calls the other girls "jerks" and "stuck-up." Your reaction is:

   a) — "All the other girls are probably wild, and Becky doesn't want to be with them because of their morals."

   b) — "Judy is an unusually perceptive girl who is as careful in choosing friends as Becky is."

   c) — "Those other girls are 'jerks' and 'stuck-up.'"

   d) — "Other young people ought to accept everyone into their circle of friendship, including Becky."

   e) — "Becky has a personality problem of some kind that we ought to check into."

   f) — "Judy is probably as desperate for friendship as Becky is."

   g) — "Other young people are selective in their friendship, and for some reason they find Becky unacceptable."

If, in situations 1 and 2 above, your checkmarks are beside *a*, *b*, *c*, and *d*, you are probably suffering from rose-sightedness. You are in no position to be of any real help to Johnny and Becky because you don't recognize a problem right before your eyes.

Avoid Rose-sightedness by Looking at Your Own Faults Realistically

Have you ever noticed how certain traits look different in ourselves than they do in other people?

You, for instance, are stubborn, but I have the courage of my convictions.

You are thin-skinned; I am sensitive.

You are rude; I just tell the truth, even if it hurts.

You are prissy; I am cultured.

You are a clothes horse; I am well-dressed.

You are overbearing; I am dynamic.

You are a spendthrift; I am generous.

You are antisocial; I am shy.

You are stingy; I am frugal.

You are cocky; I am confident.

You are prudish; I am morally sensitive.

The list could go on. We tend to see the traits of others in the darkest of colors, and our own traits in the rosiest.

This is unfortunate, because it may mean we will never correct our own errors and deficiencies. To solve our problems, we must admit we have them. To correct our mistakes, we must first of all see them.

The factory worker willing to accept criticism from his foreman will try to correct his errors. He will do better work, be in line for promotions, and gain a reputation for being cooperative and personable.

The student who accepts the teacher's red pencil marks on his English paper is far more apt to become a good writer than the one who is miffed at what that nasty old lady did to his beautiful prose.

The problem drinker will find excellent help in overcoming his problem. *If* he admits he has a problem.

The parent who honestly admits his limitations is in a far better position to rear a teenager than the parent who sees himself as the Mighty Master on All Matters of Money, Manners, and Morals.

Avoid Rose-sightedness
by Recognizing Sin as Sin

When something is black, good eyesight will see it as black.

Have you noticed how few things are called "sin" any more? There is "error" and "wrong judgment" and "maladjustment" and "social deprivation." But there is no such thing as sin.

People don't get drunk these days. They get "sopped," "inebriated," "high," "loaded," and "happy." But they don't get drunk.

Lying is "making inoperative statements."

Killing is "eliminating."

Abortion clinics don't abort; they engage in "counseling for problem pregnancies."

God, however, doesn't have the problem of rose-sightedness. He sees black as black, evil as evil.

He is "of purer eyes than to behold evil and canst not look on wrong" (Habakkuk 1:13).

"The way of the wicked is an abomination to the Lord" (Proverbs 15:9).

Satan always tries to make sin look rosy. "So when the woman saw that the tree was good for food, and that it was a delight to the eyes, and that the tree was to be desired to make one wise, she took of its fruit and ate" (Genesis 3:6).

We won't examine all the theology of that situation. Let us simply notice that Eve judged the fruit by its outward appearance. It was a "delight to the eyes." She allowed its rosy appearance to deceive her. She didn't believe that such a harmless and wholesome thing could get them evicted from their paradise. But that's exactly what happened.

Eye Exercises

To Help You Avoid Rose-sightedness

1. Take special note of any newspaper or magazine articles on how clever people use confidence schemes to trick people out of their money.

2. Try to be completely objective in deciding (a) why your son doesn't get to play much on the Little League team, (b) why your daughter didn't make the cheerleading squad, and (c) why your son doesn't get good grades in school.

3. Analyze yourself. Do you tend to be rose-sighted, or do you tend to be black-sighted? Are you more likely to be

suspicious, or more likely to be gullible?

4. Analyze yourself again. Do you often make excuses for your mistakes? Are you easily offended by criticism? If something is your fault, will you admit it?

Eye Drops

To Help Keep the Rose Out

1. "So when the woman saw that the tree was good for food, and that it was a delight to the eyes, and that the tree was to be desired to make one wise, she took of its fruit and ate."

Genesis 3:6

2. "They have healed the wound of my people lightly, saying, 'Peace, peace,' when there is no peace."

Jeremiah 6:14

3. "But Jesus would not trust himself to them, for he knew all men."

John 2:24

4. "Therefore be as shrewd as snakes and as innocent as doves. But be on your guard against men."

Matthew 10:16,17

Chapter 9
Color Blindness
(c) Green-sightedness
The Look of Envy

In the records of medical history there are few cases, if any, of green-sightedness. A few extremely color-blind people may see everything as gray, but no one sees everything as green.

Not so with the *other* eyes we have been talking about in this book. Seeing green is one of the most common ways of seeing things. Looking at others with envy and jealousy has been a major defect in mankind's visual apparatus since the beginning of his existence on earth.

Case Histories of Green-sightedness

1. When Cain and Abel brought their offerings to God, God accepted Abel's and rejected Cain's. "So Cain was very angry, and his countenance fell . . . .And when they were in the field, Cain rose up against his brother Abel, and killed him" (Genesis 4:5,8).

Cain was seeing green.

2. Sarai felt so bad at being unable to conceive that she gave her servant girl, Hagar, to Abraham. But when Hagar bore a son, Sarai began to feel different about it. "Then Sarai dealt harshly with her, and she fled from her" (Genesis 16:6).

Sarai was seeing green.

3. Jacob made for Joseph, the only son of his beloved wife Rachel, a beautiful coat with long sleeves. "But when his brothers saw that their father loved him more than all his brothers, they hated him, and could not speak peaceably to him" (Genesis 37:4).

The brothers were seeing green.

4. Miriam and Aaron, the sister and brother of Moses,

whispered to each other, "Has the Lord indeed spoken only through Moses? Has he not spoken through us also?" (Numbers 12:2).

Miriam and Aaron were seeing green.

5. After David's military victory over the Philistines, the women danced in the streets, singing, "Saul has slain his thousands, and David his ten thousands" (1 Samuel 18:7). How did King Saul respond? "And Saul was very angry, and this saying displeased him" (v. 8).

Saul was seeing green.

6. When the older brother came in from the field, he heard the sounds of a great celebration. When he was informed that the party was for his younger brother, the returned runaway, he "became angry and refused to go in" (Luke 15:28).

He was seeing green.

7. " 'Do you want me to release to you the king of the Jews?' asked Pilate, knowing it was out of envy that the chief priests had handed Jesus over to him" (Mark 15:9, 10).

The chief priests were seeing green.

8. At Pisidian Antioch, Paul and Barnabas were so popular that on the Sabbath "almost the whole city gathered to hear the word of the Lord. When the Jews saw the crowds, they were filled with jealousy and talked abusively against what Paul was saying" (Acts 13:44, 45).

They were seeing green.

9. Mark's mother brings home a new baby sister. The new baby gets all the oohs and ahs. When grandpa and grandma come over, it's to see the new baby. When the baby cries, Mom drops everything and rushes over to it. Three-year-old Mark thinks the new baby is ugly, fat, noisy, and dumb.

Mark is seeing green.

10. Mark's father observes that his wife makes every sacrifice for the new child. When the baby demands attention, the baby gets attention — no matter how late at night or how bad her headache. He is extremely proud of

his new child, but somehow there is a strange ambivalence in his feelings about her.

Mark's father is seeing green.

11. Joan is sixteen, pretty, vivacious, and athletic. Her fourteen-year-old sister, Joyce, is overweight, withdrawn, and brilliant. Joyce grits her teeth whenever she sees Joan leaving on a date with the quarterback of the football team. Joan makes a nasty comment about Joyce when she polishes off a term paper in a few hours and can spend the rest of the evening watching television.

Joyce and Joan are both seeing green.

12. The Rev. Andrew Boringsmith is critical from the pulpit about Rev. William Spectacular's new multimillion-dollar church down the street.

Pastor Boringsmith is seeing green.

13. Andy is a dentist, lives in a three-level home in a winding-road suburb, has a color TV in every bedroom, two cars, a motorcycle, and a witchy wife. His brother John is a janitor at a local high school, is making payments on an old clapboard house, owns a 1968 Chevy, goes to Friendly Joe's Loan Company at Christmas time, and has a wife who is both lovely and loving.

John sees green when he sees Andy's house, and Andy sees green when he sees John's wife.

Green-sightedness Has No Rightful Place in the Christian Life

Most of us don't think of envy as very much of a sin. After all, it doesn't kill people or even hurt them. Yet the Bible has a lot to say about that three-headed green monster, Envy-jealousy-covetousness.

It is included, for instance, in the catalog of sins in Romans 1: "Furthermore, since they did not think it worthwhile to retain the knowledge of God, he gave them over to a depraved mind, to do what ought not to be done. They have become filled with every kind of wickedness, evil, greed and depravity. They are full of envy, murder, strife, deceit and malice" (Romans 1:28,29). Here greed and envy take their place alongside depravity and murder.

In Romans 13:13 "dissension and jealousy" are listed in the same sentence as "orgies and drunkenness" and "sexual immorality and debauchery."

Time and time again the Scriptures stress that the elimination of green-sightedness is one of the signs that Christ really lives in us. Envy and all its companions have no rightful place in the Christian life.

"For since there is jealousy and quarreling among you, are you not worldly?" (1 Corinthians 3:3).

"Let us not become conceited, provoking and envying each other" (Galatians 5:26).

"At one time we too . . . lived in malice and envy, being hated and hating one another. But when the kindness and love of God our Savior appeared, he saved us" (Titus 3:3-5).

"Therefore, rid yourselves of all malice and all deceit, hypocrisy, jealousy, and slander of every kind" (1 Peter 2:1).

Eliminating Green-sightedness
Can Make Life Much More Enjoyable

Not only is green-sightedness a sin, but it also makes us miserable.

Only as this visual malady is cured can we truly begin to enjoy life.

There is enjoyment, for example, in being able to afford a new stereo or a new set of golf clubs or a new car. But the quickest way to squelch that enjoyment is to start seeing green as soon as you get it home.

You install your new ultrasonic, combination radio-record-tape stereo in the den. Then you go next door to tell your neighbor about it, only to discover that he has just purchased a new superduper hypersonic radio-record-tape stereo combination with a hundred more watts and four more woofers than yours has. Suddenly you don't like your new stereo any more. It's the same stereo that it was fifteen minutes ago, of course, but now you are seeing it through green-tinted eyes, and it has taken on a putrid color.

You save and save to buy a new white Cadillac, the top of the line with the plushest of interiors and automatic everything. Then you hear from your brother-in-law in Kalamazoo and find out he has just bought a new Mercedes Benz. Now your Cadillac looks green.

You find exactly the right evening gown at the designer shop, and you wear it with great pride at the class reunion. But five minutes after you get there you hate that gown and you wish you had never seen it. Ramona Wigglesworth is wearing the same gown — dowdy, thick, poor Ramona, the last person in the world you thought could ever afford a dress like that.

And so it continues.

The problem is that no matter how much we have, there will always be a few people who have it better. And as long as we keep seeing green, we'll never be able to enjoy what we have.

One of the secrets of happiness is contentment. No one can ever be content if he is afflicted with the color blindness that continually sees green.

When we learn to enjoy what we have *without comparing it with what others have*, then we have learned one of the secrets of successful living.

"I have learned the secret of being content in any and every situation, whether well-fed or hungry, whether living in plenty or in want. I can do everything through him who gives me strength" (Philippians 4:12, 13).

Concentrate on What You Are
Rather Than What You Have

What we *are* will be with us for all of this life and for all eternity. What we *have* may or may not be with us for this life, but we know for certain it will not be with us in the life to come.

Be not afraid when one becomes rich,
  when the glory of his house increases.
For when he dies he will carry nothing away;
  his glory will not go down after him.

Psalm 49:16,17

Why see green over something that will pass away?

That is why Jesus said, "Do not store up for yourselves treasures on earth, where moth and rust destroy, and where thieves break in and steal. But store up for yourselves treasures in heaven, where moth and rust do not destroy, and where thieves do not break in and steal" (Matthew 6:19,20).

Practice the Art of Thanksgiving

The best cure for green-sightedness is a good dose of thanksgiving at least three times a day.

Paul said to Timothy, "For everything God created is good, and nothing is to be rejected if it is received with thanksgiving, because it is consecrated by the word of God and prayer" (1 Timothy 4:4).

When a person is thankful, he is concentrating on what he has rather than on what he doesn't have.

When a person is thankful, he is looking upward to God rather than around at the possessions of his fellow men.

When a person is thankful, he is counting his blessings, not his deficits.

When a person is thankful, he is acknowledging the grace of God rather than the stinginess of people.

When a person is thankful, he is holding his hand out to receive, not thrusting his hand forward to grab.

Practice the Art of Loving

Envy is a first cousin of those torturous triplets, Malice, Anger, and Hatred. It is difficult to like the people we are envious of.

Green-sightedness is soon followed by red-sightedness. If we see green when we see our neighbor's possessions, we will then see red when we see our neighbor.

In fact, envy can lead to violence and even murder. The stories of Cain and Abel, Joseph and his brothers, Saul and David, and Jesus and the priests are examples of that.

Thus one of the obvious ways to counteract green-sightedness is to genuinely love one another.

"Love is patient, love is kind. It does not envy, it does not boast, it is not proud" (1 Corinthians 13:4).

To love is to seek the best for another, despite what our personal feelings might be.

To love is to weep with those who weep and to rejoice with those who rejoice. And to be honest — isn't it easier to weep with those who weep than it is to rejoice with those who rejoice? When we're all in the same race, it's easier to be sympathetic with the last-place finisher than it is to celebrate with the winner.

To really love is to do both. When we do that, we squeeze out envy.

Eye Exercises

To Take the Green Out

1. Every morning for an entire month write down one thing or person you are thankful for. Make the list specific. Each day include in your prayers a special thanks for each item.

2. Memorize your "Eye Drops" faithfully. Review those of the last chapter.

3. Sincerely congratulate someone who has succeeded at something you have not (suggestions: an election winner, someone who has purchased a larger house, a contest winner, someone who received a promotion, someone who received better grades).

4. The next time a neighbor gets a new dining room set, riding lawnmower, or garbage compactor, decide *not* to get one for yourself.

Eye Drops

To Help Take Away the Green

1. "Be still before the Lord, and wait patiently for him; fret not yourself over him who prospers in his way."

Psalm 37:7

2. "I have learned the secret of being content in any and every situation, whether well-fed or hungry, whether living in plenty or in want."

Philippians 4:12

3. "Love is patient, love is kind. It does not envy, it does not boast, it is not proud."

1 Corinthians 13:4

4. "Let us not become conceited, provoking and envying each other."

Galatians 5:26

Chapter 10

Tunnel Vision

The term *tunnel vision* is remarkably self-explanatory. The person with tunnel vision sees as if he were on the inside of a tunnel looking out. He can see straight ahead, but all else is blurred or dark.

Some Other Creatures Don't Have It

Many of God's other creatures see more broadly and widely than humans do.

Fish, for instance, have eyes on opposite sides of their heads, enabling them to see in a 360-degree sweep.

The fiddler crab also has a remarkable ability. His eyes are on stalks, and when buried in the sand, he can raise them like periscopes to scan his entire surroundings.

The tropical fish anableps has the world's first bifocals, which enable him to see above the water and below the water at the same time. Each eye has two pupils: When he swims along the surface of the water, one set of pupils looks upward into the air and the other looks downward into the water.

The owl has eyes so large that they cannot turn in their sockets. But he can swivel his head in such a way that he can see directly backward.

Human Eyes and Peripheral Vision

Human eyes are more limited in their scope.

The vertical range of your eyes is about 140 degrees. Your brows prevent you from looking directly upward, and your cheeks prevent you from looking directly downward.

Your horizontal range is a bit more impressive, about 180 degrees. Each of your eyes has a range of about 150 degrees. Where the fields of vision overlap you have binocular vision, or depth perception. This is the area of direct focus.

The vision that you have outside this area is called peripheral vision. You might call it "seeing out of the corner of my eyes."

What you see out of the corner of your eyes may not be in focus or in three dimensions, but it is important to you nevertheless. When you are driving a car, for example, you concentrate on the traffic immediately in front of you. But your peripheral vision enables you to see a car coming onto the highway from a side street, and hopefully you are able to swerve to avoid an accident.

Anyone engaged in team sports uses peripheral vision continually. The quarterback, for instance, focuses on one or two potential receivers, but his peripheral vision enables him to see the 250-pound bone-crusher thundering upon him from the side.

Tunnel vision is eyesight deprived of peripheral vision. The person with tunnel vision can focus on objects of his choice, but he is not conscious of the surrounding landscape. He does not notice the automobile, nor the defensive end about to crash into his right flank.

We might say that such a person has narrow vision. His field of vision is very limited. He cannot see to the right or to the left, or to the top or to the bottom. He can see only where he wants to see.

Narrow-mindedness

Actually not many people are afflicted with tunnel vision — that is, the tunnel vision of the physical eyes.

But many more people are afflicted with the tunnel vision of the mental and spiritual eyes. They are narrow-minded.

You recognize such a person readily, He says thing like,

"My mind is made up. Don't disturb me with facts."

Not only does he have strong convictions, but he believes everyone else ought to have exactly the same convictions. You'd like to debate with him, but you know it's no use.

He has been overheard saying, "The Bible is so crystal clear on that particular teaching that I don't see how you can believe anything else."

He tends, you see, to equate what he *believes* the Bible says with what the Bible says.

He has been known to admit the possibility he might be wrong, but he considers it highly unlikely.

Worst of all, he can be extremely critical of others. He not only accepts his own conceptions as true, but he rejects all others as false. And not only are they false, but they are "blatant lies" and "teachings of Satan." He considers his point of view far more important than the inward harmony of the body of Christ. He will raise such a fuss about how a toenail is trimmed that eventually the entire body becomes immobilized.

The tragic results of religious narrow-mindedness are not limited to the church, however, as Jonathan Swift points out in his caustic satire of humanity, *Gulliver's Travels*.

While Gulliver is visiting Lilliput, the country of little people, he is told that Lilliput is at war with Blefuscu, the "other great empire of the universe." The cause: a feud between the Big-Endians and the Little-Endians. The Big-Endians believe an egg ought to be broken at the big end, and the Little-Endians believe it should be broken on the little end. War has been declared, and over a period of three years Lilliput alone has lost forty ships and thirty thousand men. Each party has written hundreds of books defending its position and quotes from its mutual holy book the verse, "That all true believers break their eggs at the convenient end."

We wish we could say that Swift has overstated his case against religious bigotry. We can't.

The president of a Christian college forbids his students to attend the crusades of a traveling evangelist, under threat of expulsion.

One Christian college sends out a rock-and-roll group to give programs and testimonies, and another Christian college condemns rock-and-roll as "of the devil."

The Baptists shake their heads at those poor benighted Lutherans who burn all those candles; and the Lutherans shake their heads at those unbalanced Baptists who say "amen" aloud in church.

First Fundamentalist Church condemns all card-playing as Satan-inspired, and First High Church sees nothing wrong with playing bingo to raise money for the building fund.

The members of Trinity Church must vow total abstinence from alcoholic beverages, but after church they puff on cigarettes like choo-choo trains; and the members of Grace Church condemn tobacco but serve liquor at church socials.

A teenager constantly criticizes his father's pollution-dumping plant, and the father's dinner conversation consists of nine words: "When are you going to get your hair cut?"

The chairman of the music committee thinks Gospel songs are the only way to really express one's spiritual feelings. He is having a running feud with the organist, who believes that God much prefers to hear the music of Bach and Beethoven.

At First Church the charismatics are at war with the noncharismatics; at Second Church the premillenarians are engaged in a bitter dispute with the postmillenarians; and at Third Church the free-willers are in a seesaw battle with the electionists.

The Seventh-day Adventists say the Sabbath ought to

be observed on Saturday, and most mainstream Protestants and Roman Catholics observe Sunday as the Lord's Day.

Some Christian groups today do not allow any kind of "worldly" activity on Sunday — including boating, golfing, mowing lawns, picnicking, swimming, movies, or shopping. Other groups see nothing wrong with any of these activities, making no real distinction between Sunday and any other day of the week.

Some Ancient Tunnels

Tunnel vision in the church is nothing new, of course.

The Pharisees criticized Jesus and His disciples for not washing their bowls properly, for healing on the Sabbath, and for a host of other infractions that they considered major crimes.

The early church also had more than its share of controversies. One of them raged over the issue of keeping a holy day. "One man considers one day more sacred than another; another man considers every day alike" (Romans 14:5). This controversy is far from new!

Another issue that had the potential for causing trouble was what food Christians could eat. This matter became a rather sharp one in the church at Corinth (see 1 Corinthians 8:1-3). In that pagan city almost all the meat sold in the public market had first been offered to idols in a slaughter ritual. Some Christians had no spiritual problem in eating it because they neither participated in the ceremony nor believed in idols. Others, however, had guilt feelings about it because they believed that somehow they were participating in a pagan ceremony, no matter how indirectly.

It becomes obvious that certain kinds of tunnel vision have a bad effect on our personal relationships and can cause bad feelings among Christians. Tunnel vision can result in divisions in the church.

How can we avoid developing tunnel vision in these

matters? How can we avoid being too narrow-minded on one hand, and too wishy-washy on the other?

Here are a few suggestions.

Let Us Learn to Tell the Difference
Between Core Matters and Peripheral Matters

In some ways, biblical teaching is narrow.

"How long will you go limping with two different opinions? If the Lord is God, follow him; but if Baal, then follow him" (1 Kings 18:21).

"No one can serve two masters. Either he will hate the one and love the other, or he will be devoted to the one and hate the other" (Matthew 6:24).

"I am the way — and the truth and the life" (John 14:6).

On the essentials of the faith we ought not to yield an inch. On the basics there is no compromise. The salvation of souls and the integrity of the Christian religion are at stake.

But we must recognize the fact that not everything is essential. Not all matters are of equal importance. Some beliefs are at the core of the faith, and some beliefs are at the outer edges of the circle.

"Food does not bring us near to God; we are no worse if we do not eat, and no better if we do" (1 Corinthians 8:8).

Nor does the Bible say, in so many words, which day we should keep. Some, indeed, might debate whether we are duty-bound to keep any day at all. (See Romans 14:5.) Let us recognize that the keeping of the holy day is at the periphery of the faith and not the core of it. If it were of essential and utmost importance to Him, God would have made it much more clear in His Word.

Does the Bible really specify how long a man's hair ought to be? Or a boy's? A woman's? A girl's?

Does it say what kind of church music is acceptable to God? Or whether ballads are better than rock-and-roll? Whether symphonic music is better to play on Christian radio stations than is the hit parade?

108

Does not the Bible teach *both* election and human responsibility?

Does the Bible either condemn or approve movie-going?

Is it all that important to know the pre-history of the end-time?

Does the Bible say that the styles of the 1800s were better than those of the present? Or that those of the 1950s were more godly than those of the 1970s? Does it decree what color our clothing ought to be? Or how short our skirts? How bare our chests?

Does God promote either vegetarianism or carnivorism?

Did Jesus put His seal of approval on either silent meditation or wild hand-clapping? Do they rule each other out?

"For the kingdom of God is not a matter of eating and drinking, but of righteousness, peace and joy in the Holy Spirit" (Romans 14:17).

There you have it!

There are some core matters: "righteousness, peace, and joy in the Holy Spirit." These three things are most important of all: one's basic ethics; one's inner relationship to God; and one's sense of spiritual well-being. These are more important than whether a person prefers Monopoly or Crazy-eight.

Jesus said, "But seek first his kingdom and his righteousness, and all these things will be given to you as well" (Matthew 6:33). To make God the King of our lives — that is most important. When we do that, the other things will fall into place.

Let Us Live in Such a Way That It Enhances Our Walk With the Lord

"As one who is in the Lord Jesus, I am fully convinced that no food is unclean in itself. But if anyone regards something as unclean, then for him it is unclean" (Romans 14:14).

109

"Some people are still so accustomed to idols that when they eat such meat, they think of it as having been sacrificed to an idol, and since their conscience is weak, it is defiled" (1 Corinthians 8:7).

If, after having examined your own conscience in the light of Scripture, you believe that your voluntary observance of a certain practice is what God wishes you to do, then by all means do it.

You are not obligated to yield to the opinions and pressures of others (any more than they are obligated to yield to yours).

The important thing is that you examine your views in the light of Scripture and that you act accordingly.

Let Us, in Love, Strive to Build Up the Christian Community

The worst thing about tunnel vision is that it can become a divisive factor in the Christian community.

The Scripture is most emphatic when it states that the Christian's first obligation in these controversial matters is to maintain the unity of the body of Christ. Even when there are differences of opinion there is to be love and consideration for other believers.

"The man who eats everything must not look down on him who does not, and the man who does not eat everything must not condemn the man who does, for God has accepted him. Who are you to judge someone else's servant?" (Romans 14:3, 4).

"You, then, why do you judge your brother? Or why do you look down on your brother? For we will all stand before God's judgment seat" (v. 10).

"If your brother is distressed because of what you eat, you are no longer acting in love. Do not by your eating destroy your brother for whom Christ died" (v. 15).

"Let us therefore make every effort to do what leads to peace and to mutual edification" (v. 19).

"It is better not to eat meat or drink wine or to do

anything else that will cause your brother to fall" (v. 21).

One day a lawyer asked Jesus, "Teacher, which is the greatest commandment in the Law?" (Matthew 22:36).

He had tunnel vision, you see. He no doubt had picked out one of the ten commandments as his very own favorite, and he loved to nit-pick about it.

But Jesus refused to approve the lawyer's way of looking at things. "Jesus replied: 'Love the Lord your God with all your heart, with all your soul and with all your mind.' This is the first and greatest commandment. And the second is like it: 'Love your neighbor as yourself' " (vv. 37-39).

Love, He was saying, is even more important than the letter of the law. The law is meaningful only if kept in the spirit of love.

Love broadens one's outlook considerably. As the RSV translates it, "Love does not insist on its own way" (1 Corinthians 13:5).

Love is being willing to be an usher, even though the head usher vetoed your strong conviction that ushers ought to wear white boutonnieres.

Love is being willing to be in the Mother's Day program, even though the committee didn't choose the one you had written.

Love is giving our Christian brothers and sisters "breathing room."

We all need room to be different, room to disagree, room to have varying opinions, room to exercise our own personalities, room to display our idiosyncrasies, room even to observe our own irrational taboos.

We must create a Christian community where there is no fear of having our toes stepped on if they stray an inch over the line.

Let us be broad-minded enough to see that in the absence of clear direction in the Word, sincere born-again believers can have widely differing views on many practices.

Let us be smart enough to realize that many of our ideas

111

about observances, styles, and recreation come from parental influences, cultural backgrounds, and church traditions rather than directly from the Bible.

Let us not confuse preference with piety, or culture with conviction.

Let us be able to look to the right of us and see sincere Christians who are far more strict about some things than we are, without ridiculing them for it.

Let us be able to look to the left of us and see sincere Christians who are far more liberal than we are, without feeling superior to them for it.

Let us, in short, overcome tunnel vision with love.

Eye Exercises

To Help Prevent Tunnel Vision

Take a few current differences of opinion . . .

Long male hair/short male hair
A popular dance/the Charleston
Johann Sebastian Bach/Fanny Crosby
Amillenarianism/premillenarianism
Female head covered/female head uncovered
Strict Sunday observance/non-strict Sunday observance
Short female hair/long female hair
Formal worship service/informal worship service

_____

_____

_____

. . . and ask these questions about your attitudes:

1. Is this at the core or the periphery of the faith?
2. Does the Bible give any definitive directions?
3. Are you maintaining your own personal convictions?
4. Does your attitude toward those who differ with you encourage or discourage Christian fellowship?
5. To what extent are your opinions influenced by your age?

6. Do the opinions you express publicly on the subject detract from or enhance your Christian witness?
7. Can you maintain a good personal relationship with someone who disagrees with you on this matter?

Eye Drops

To Enlarge the Scope of Your Vision

1. "For the kingdom of God is not a matter of eating and drinking, but of righteousness, peace, and joy in the Holy Spirit."

Romans 14:17

2. "You, then, why do you judge your brother? Or why do you look down on your brother? For we will all stand before God's judgment seat."

Romans 14:10

3. " 'Love the Lord your God with all your heart, with all your soul and with all your mind.' This is the first and greatest commandment. And the second is like it: 'Love your neighbor as yourself.' "

Matthew 22:37-39

4. "Let us therefore make every effort to do what leads to peace and to mutual edification."

Romans 14:19

Chapter 11

Limited Vision

The human eye is a marvelous, miraculous organ. Comparing it with the very best of precision cameras is like comparing the Taj Mahal with a tarpaper shack. Yet the eye has its limitations. There are things it simply cannot do.

Human eyes, for instance, cannot do what some chameleon eyes can do — swivel independently of each other like gun turrets on a battleship.

Our eyes are more limited than those of fish, because their eyes are placed on opposite sides of the head, enabling the fish to see a full 360 degrees.

They are not so versatile as those of the fiddler crab, who can bury himself under the sand and raise his eyes on stalks, like two periscopes.

Nor can we, like hawks, spot a rabbit hopping through the underbrush a thousand feet below.

We cannot see around corners or see in complete darkness or see through opaque objects.

Nor can we, in fact, see most of the electromagnetic waves that are all around us. We are blind to all except a minute percent of the spectrum. A chart of waves in the "L" volume of the World Book Encyclopedia is 9¼ inches long. Of this list, visible light is less than a quarter-inch long. Our eyes are simply not equipped to see cosmic rays, gamma rays, x-rays, ultraviolet rays, infrared rays, radio waves, or electric current.

Truly our vision is limited.

What is true of our physical eyesight is also true of our

capacity to comprehend other realities in the universe. There are many things that our finite beings are simply not designed to fully understand.

God, in His divine wisdom, has deliberately curtailed our power of perception. Some things are impossible for us to see.

We may complain about this handicap, and we may try to devise extraordinary means to overcome it — but the truth is that we are better off the way we are.

What are some of the limitations of our vision?

We Are Limited in Our Vision of God

"No man has ever seen God," say John's Gospel (1:18).

God is so difficult to visualize. How do you imagine a spirit looks?

We know He's not an old man with a beard. But it's hard to dismiss that image because we have nothing better to replace it with. One youth told the author that he imagined God as a great, radiant white blob.

We chafe sometimes at the limited concept we have of the Almighty. It seems unfair that our concept of God is so limited. But really, don't you think it's much better that way? What do you suppose would happen if we could see God in all His splendor and glory?

Do you remember the warnings we received during the eclipse of the sun in 1970? We were told again and again not to look at the sun without the aid of dark, smoked glass. The sun, we were informed, could blind us even in one quick glance.

We have reason to believe that the glory of God makes the sun look like a night light in comparison. Our feeble natures simply could not survive the full experience of God.

The Book of Exodus gives us a homey yet vivid story of this truth. Moses, too, wanted to see the fullness of God.

"I pray thee," he said, "show me thy glory" (Exodus 33:18).

And God said,

> "You cannot see my face; for man shall not see me and live." And the Lord said, "Behold, there is a place where you shall stand upon the rock; and while my glory passes by I will put you in a cleft of the rock, and I will cover you with my hand until I have passed by; then I will take away my hand, and you shall see my back; but my face shall not be seen."

Exodus 33:20-23

"Man shall not see me and live." God has given us a limited vision of Himself simply because 20/20 vision would kill us.

Does this mean we are unable to comprehend God at all?

Of course not. God allows Himself to be known by at least three means: (1) His mighty acts, (2) the world He has created, and (3) His Son, Jesus Christ.

Let's look at these three means.

1. God allows Himself to be seen by us *through His mighty acts of love*.

In this same conversation, God told Moses there would be ample evidence of His existence: "I will make all my goodness pass before you, and will proclaim before you my name 'The LORD'; and I will be gracious to whom I will be gracious, and will show mercy on whom I will show mercy" (Exodus 33:19).

God cited here four evidences that Moses could see: (a) "my goodness," (b) "my name," (c) graciousness, and (d) mercy. These attributes of God's personality unfolded throughout the entire history of Israel, from the calling of Abraham to such events as the deliverance from the slavery of Egypt and the entrance into the Promised Land.

Has God performed mighty acts of love in your life? If He has, you have plenty of evidence that He exists, though you have never seen Him with your eyes.

2. God also allows Himself to be seen by us *through nature*.

116

Romans 1:20 says, "For since the creation of the world God's invisible qualities — his eternal power and divine nature — have been clearly seen, being understood from what has been made, so that men are without excuse."

We may not see His glory directly, but we can see it indirectly in the fantastic energy of a billion suns.

We may not be able to comprehend fully His vast wisdom and knowledge, but we can catch a fleeting glimpse of it in the unbelievable complexity of a single atom.

We may not be able to visualize His beauty, but we can see a twinkle of it in the dewy whiteness of a lily of the valley.

3. Most importantly, God has enabled us to visualize Him *through His Son, Jesus Christ.*

In opening this chapter with a quote from John 1:18, we quoted only part of the sentence. The entire verse reads like this: "No man has ever seen God, but God the only Son, who is at the Father's side, has made him known."

Paul echoes this truth when he says God has given us "the light of the knowledge of the glory of God in the face of Christ" (2 Corinthians 4:6).

If you wished to communicate with ants, what would be the most effective way of doing it? Become an ant.

That's how God chose to communicate with us: He became one of us.

He shared our language so He could speak to us face to face.

He shared our hurts, sorrows, and difficulties, so He could sympathize with us.

He shared our temptations so He could help us.

Most of all, He shared our guilt (though not our sin), so He could be punished for it on our behalf.

An electrical transformer takes the high-voltage electricity from the high line and reduces it to a level we can safely use. Jesus Christ is, in a sense, God's transformer. As an electrical transformer harnesses the killer-volts of surging electricity so they can be used for toasters and air

117

conditioners, so Jesus Christ harnessed the fantastic power of the Almighty and used it to make blind men see, lame men walk, and dumb men speak. The "glory of God in the face of Christ" was far more safe and useful than the glory from which God shielded Moses in the wilderness.

Because the language of heaven is too ethereal for human ears to hear, and too transcendant for human minds to understand, Jesus of Nazareth talked in Aramaic about birds of the air, a boy who ran away from home, and a sheep that got lost.

The limitations of the eye — yes, it is true that the human perception cannot comprehend the full Being of God.

But God has revealed Himself in His mighty acts, in nature, and in His Son. We don't know all there is to know about Him (if we did we would be Gods), but we know all that it is necessary to know. We know how to be saved and we know how we ought to live. We know how to conduct ourselves in this life and how successfully to make the transition to the next one.

What else do we really need to see?

We Have Limited Vision in Seeing the Reason for Tragedy and Hardship

Remember the story of Job? He had been one of the wealthiest men in that part of the country. Then the Sabeans stole his oxen and asses; fire from heaven burned up his sheep; the Chaldeans rustled his camels, and all his servants were killed in the process. A wind demolished the house where his seven sons and three daughters were having a party, killing them all. And finally Job himself was covered with great sores over all his body.

All he had left was a nagging wife.

Oh yes, he also had three friends with all kinds of smart theories about what had happened. Their favorite line was that God was punishing Job for some heinous secret sin, and that the sooner he got it off his chest the better.

"Those who plow iniquity and sow trouble reap the same" (Job 4:8).

The intricacies of their thirty-four chapter discussion as to the why and wherefore of evil are too long and involved to be traced here. After endless hours of speculation, argument, surmise, philosophy, psychology, and other sorts of mental gymnastics, God breaks into the conversation and asks Job a few questions:

"Where were you when I laid the foundation of the earth?" (38:4)

"Who determined its measurements — surely you know!" (v. 5)

"Who shut in the sea with doors?" (v. 8)

"Where is the way to the dwelling of light?" (v. 19)

"Is it by your wisdom that the hawk soars?" (39:26)

"Shall a faultfinder contend with the Almighty?" (40:2)

"Will you condemn me that you may be justified?" (v. 8)

In summary, God was saying to Job: "Job, you are a man and I am God. You are simply not equipped to understand these things. You cannot even comprehend the mysteries of the world you can see; how can you expect to comprehend the mysteries of the world you cannot see? Job, your vision is limited. You cannot possibly see the reason for the tragedies that have befallen you. But I, as God, am all-powerful and all-seeing; and I know all the reasons. Job, as you have trusted and served me in the past, continue to do so in the future, no matter what happens. You're in good hands with Jehovah."

Job realized — as we must realize — that he had been wrong in criticizing God for something he did not understand. Then Job answered, "I have uttered what I did not understand, things too wonderful for me, which I did not know . . . therefore I despise myself, and repent in dust and ashes" (42:3,6).

In a way, that's not very satisfying. We all like to have answers that are both immediate and complete. We dislike loose ends. We want to be able to say, "I know the reason why Uncle Joe has cancer," and "I can tell you exactly why Patricia is paralyzed from her neck down, and why little Bobby was born with a congenital heart ailment."

There are times, of course, when the reasons for tragedies and near-tragedies become apparent right away. A traveling salesman from Illinois was involved in an automobile accident ten miles from his home. His wife rushed to the hospital, saying over and over again, "Why, why, why?" Within the space of two years the family had suffered three major surgeries, a financial setback, a heart attack, and spiritual concern over a daughter. And now this. Why?

The answer came that very day. The man was x-rayed in the hospital. No broken bones. But the doctors discovered a spot on the left lung. Surgery the next day removed the tumor, which if not discovered could have become malignant and probably terminal. They knew the reason why.

But this is the exception rather than the rule. Most answers do not come so quickly, and many of them never come at all.

If having limited vision is frustrating and irritating, then being misguided in one's vision can be downright terrifying.

Remember Job's three friends? They had things all figured out. If Job would only confess his secret sin, his troubles would be over. As if all Job's problems weren't already bad enough, they tried to add a heaping dose of guilt. The proposed medicine was almost as lethal as the illness it was supposed to cure.

That's a problem today with a lot of so-called friends. They tell the arthritis sufferer that if only she had enough faith she would be cured. They tell the woman on the verge of an emotional collapse that if she had walked more closely with the Lord this wouldn't have happened. They tell the single girl who has had a miscarriage that God is punishing her for her sin. They say it is unbelief that is keeping a paralyzed man from walking again.

The God who limited Job's vision (and ours) was more merciful than the friends who thought they could help him to see everything.

As a pastor I have been asked again and again, "Why?" "Why did my child die?" "Why does the eighty-seven-year-old vegetable continue to live, but a beautiful bride is killed in an auto accident?" "Why am I afflicted with this nervous condition?" "Why?" "Why?" "Why?"

I wish I could give an answer — a nice, easy, affirmative, final, authoritative answer. But I can't and won't pretend to. I won't even speculate. We have to leave the answers with God. We have limited vision, but His vision knows no boundaries.

> For my thoughts are not your thoughts,
> neither are your ways my ways, says the Lord.
> For as the heavens are higher than the earth,
> so are my ways higher than your ways
> and my thoughts than your thoughts.
> *Isaiah 55:8,9*

It would be nice always to be able to walk on a brightly lighted path. But in the absence of that luxury it is best to put one's hand in the hand of Him who sees in the dark, before whom there is no night, in whose mind there are no questions, and in whose future there are no mysteries.

We look, then, to the day in the future, in the life to come, when these old, limited eyes will be replaced by spiritual eyes that are far, far more perceptive. Then and then alone will our limited vision be corrected. It will not be by corrective lenses or by eye medication, but by a radical transplant, a substitution of the new spiritual eyes for the old physical eyes.

The eyes are a part of that body which "is sown in weakness," but will be "raised in power" (1 Corinthians 15:43). "It is sown a natural body, it is raised a spiritual body" (v. 44). The eyes of the physical body are limited, but the eyes of the spiritual body will be able to share in

121

spiritual perception. "Now we see but a poor reflection; then we shall see face to face" (1 Corinthians 13:12).

Many Unscrupulous People Are Eager to Help Us See Into the Future

As greedy men offer fortune-gobbling fake cures to desperate cancer victims, so greedy men offer expensive eye remedies to desperate people who want to see into the future.

Undaunted by Jeane Dixon's prediction that Jacqueline Kennedy would never marry again — published on the day of Jackie's marriage to Aristotle Onassis — thousands of vulnerable people continue to believe in Ms. Dixon's bold assertions as gospel truth.

Palmists, crystal-gazers, mystics, séance peddlers — they're standing in line to help you see into the future. And some will even let you use your Mastercharge.

Twelve hundred American newspapers carry regular astrology columns. If one should neglect to run the column for a day it is deluged by angry calls from hundreds of people. Ten million Americans read the astrology forecasts more religiously than they read their Bibles, plunking down a $150 million a year for the privilege of doing so.

The words of God through Isaiah the prophet have a strangely contemporary sound:

> You are wearied with your many counsels;
> let them stand forth and save you,
> those who divide the heavens,
> who gaze at the stars,
> who at the new moons predict
> what shall befall you.
>
> *Isaiah 47:13*

God, through Moses, gives some rather strong warnings to His people about the temptation to use mystical practices in an effort to gain foreknowledge of the future: "There shall not be found among you . . . any one who practices divination, a soothsayer, or an augur, or a sorcerer, or a charmer, or a medium, or a wizard, or a necromancer. For whoever does these things is an abomination to the Lord" (Deuteronomy 18:10-12).

You don't really want to be an "abomination," do you?

God Is Merciful by Giving Us Limited Vision

Jesus said, "Therefore do not worry about tomorrow, for tomorrow will worry about itself. Each day has enough trouble of its own" (Matthew 6:34).

That's the principle: Each day's challenge is sufficient for itself. We have a hard-enough time coping with today, much less trying to cope with tomorrow at the same time. In today's complicated and competitive world, we have all we can do to handle each day as it comes.

Thus God in His wisdom has shielded us from knowledge of tomorrow. We simply wouldn't be up to it. We are given limited vision because we have limited resources.

There is enough tension working for the present boss, without having the knowledge that within a week you'll be getting a worse one.

It is difficult to pay each month's bills now. But it would be even more painful if you knew in advance that you are going to get laid off within six months.

The limitations on our vision have been placed there by the goodness of God.

It's His way of saying that we ought to live by faith, not by sight alone. We are to live by hope, not by complete knowledge.

Our strength is not in knowing all about tomorrow, but in knowing the God of tomorrow.

Eye Exercises

To Help You Cope With Limited Vision

1. When someone asks you what your astrological sign is, answer, "It really doesn't interest me in the least. The

123

position of the planets on the day of my birth has no influence on what I do with today."

2. When trying to comfort someone who has suffered hardship or tragedy, squelch the temptation to give a glib explanation to the question "Why?"

3. On a piece of paper write down five things you most often worry about. Then analyze them. Do you worry more about the present or about the future? If you worry about the future, how much good does it do? Set your list alongside Matthew 6:34. Now would you like to revise your list?

4. Engage a Christian friend in a discussion about your respective mental images of what God is like. Can you have widely different mental images and still be believing in and worshiping the same God? Discuss what you both think is the most important thing to remember about your concepts of God.

Eye Drops

For Those Troubled by Their Limited Vision

1. "For my thoughts are not your thoughts,
   neither are your ways my ways, says the Lord.
For as the heavens are higher than the earth,
   so are my ways higher than your ways,
   and my thoughts than your thoughts."
Isaiah 55:8,9

2. "Shall a faultfinder contend with the Almighty?"
Job 40:2a

3. "No man has ever seen God, but God the only Son, who is at the Father's side, has made him known."
John 1:18

4. "Now we see but a poor reflection; then we shall see face to face." *1 Corinthians 13:12a*

Chapter 12

Suggestions for Group Leaders

Chapter 1 — Divine Ophthalmology

1. Encourage the members of the group to commit the "Eye Drops" to memory before each meeting. You may wish to have them say the verses in unison as a class. Or, you may wish to call on individuals to recite them before the group.

Demonstrate how to make flash cards with these verses. Write the Scripture reference and perhaps the first few words on one side of a three-by-five card, and write the full verse on the other side. Encourage the group members to carry the cards with them and to drill with them at convenient spare moments throughout the day.

2. Bring to class some pictures that illustrate how the eyes and the mind can play tricks on the individual. You might use some of the common optical illusions frequently used to demonstrate this phenomenon ("Which line is the longer?" etc.). Or, you may be able to find photographs similar to the ones mentioned in the book (two-headed camel and huge man on boat).

This same suggestion is found in the "Eye Exercises" for chapter 1, so your class members may also remember to bring such pictures to class.

3. Conduct a discussion on 2 Corinthians 5:16,17. In what ways does being a Christian change our viewpoint of others? What are characteristics of the "worldly" point of view? In what ways do the Christian's views of Christ differ from the world's views?

4. Secure from a local optometrist, ophthalmologist, or schoolteacher a large diagram of the eye. Use it to arouse interest in your class, and refer to it from time to time in the course of your lectures and discussion.

5. Point out the truth of 1 Corinthians 13:12, "Now we see but a poor reflection; then we shall see face to face." Our eyesight will never be perfect in this lifetime, but we look to the new spiritual eyes which we shall receive in the life to come.

Chapter 2 — Blindness

1. There may be someone in your circle of friends and acquaintances who is blind and who will be willing to give a short testimony. He may also have some hints as to what kind of help blind people appreciate and what kind they don't care to have.

2. Illustrations of how people can be blind to oncoming destruction: (1) The people of Jerusalem were unaware of the terrible destruction which they would suffer at the hands of Rome in A.D. 70 (see Luke 19:41,42); (2) The United States was blind to the attack on Pearl Harbor. Even though the Japanese planes were detected on radar, the warning was disregarded. Let us not be blind to the judgment of God.

3. Discuss some personal kinds of blindness:
   a) Blindness to a child's need for love
   b) Blindness to a loved one's need for communication and understanding
   c) Blindness to growing resentment by employees
   d) Blindness to poverty, discrimination, and despair all around us

4. Evaluate with your group your church's ministry to (a) the physically blind, and (b) the spiritually blind. What is the relationship between the two? Consider Jesus' ministry to both needs. Is the church's ministry to be entirely physical? Is the church's ministry to be entirely spiritual?

5. Close the meeting with the hymn, "The Light of the World Is Jesus."

Chapter 3 — **Myopia**

1. Find examples of other great men and women who had a vision and a goal far beyond that of most of their contemporaries, persons who set out to achieve what others thought impossible. Examples: explorers, civil rights leaders, inventors, revolutionaries, architects, musicians, religious leaders. You may wish to assign short reports to class members.

2. Evaluate Dr. Martin Luther King's famous "I Have a Dream" speech in light of this chapter. Likewise, the Declaration of Independence.

3. The philosophy "I take each day as it comes" is a popular one. In what way is it a good one? In what way can it be a bad way to view life?

4. As a practical application of this lesson, have your group draw up a number of long-range goals for itself. If your organization already has such a statement or constitution, study it to see if it is up to date. You may wish to formulate some new goals. If there is general consensus, refer the matter to the executive committee or a special committee for the final formulation.

Spend some time discussing together the "Eye Exercises" in this lesson.

6. Keep reminding the group about the "Eye Drops."

Chapter 4 — **Hyperopia**

1. Did your group compile a number of long-range goals and guiding principles, as suggested in the last chapter? If you did, good. But if you allow those high ideals just to sit there as high ideals, your group might get a bad case of hyperopia!

So, to prevent that dread disease, write your goals on the board and ask for suggestions on how you can reach them. After agreeing on which of these practical measures to use, begin to take practical steps to implement them. Appoint committees, assign responsibilities, and appropriate necessary funds.

2. Review your church budget, taking special note of two items: (a) How much are you spending to alleviate poverty on far-away mission fields? and (b) How much are you spending to alleviate poverty in your own community? How do you determine a proper balance?

3. Discuss these two questions and their implications: (a) Are you supporting mission programs among black people in Africa? (b) How would you react if black people applied for membership in your church?

4. Following up on no. 6 of the "Eye Exercises," ask the group members to tell about things they observed on their way to today's meeting.

Chapter 5 — Getting Used to the Dark

1. Bring clippings to the class that illustrate the principle which is the theme of the chapter. You may find such items as Gallup polls, magazine surveys, editorials, or interviews. (This suggestion is also made in "Eye Exercises," so get your class to participate in this.)

2. Discuss: Does change mean progress? On the other hand, does it mean regress? There are those who resist change of any kind, and there are others who blindly advocate any change for the sake of change. What is a good position that avoids these two extremes? On what basis do we determine whether change is good or bad?

3. Discuss questions 2 and 4 in "Eye Exercises."

4. Further illustration: The individual frames of a moving picture are very little different from those ahead of it and behind it. In fact, the difference is almost indistinguishable by the naked eye. Only when they are shown in fast sequence can the movement be seen. But the movement is significant, nevertheless.

5. Further information: It is estimated that the typical American adult views television 6.5 hours per day and reads the newspaper 32 minutes per day. Through these and other means, such as billboards, radio, and mail circulars, he is exposed to more than 500 (yes, five

hundred) advertising messages a day. Question: How many of these are we conscious of? How many of these have an effect on us without our knowledge?

6. Discuss some personal ways in which people can get used to the dark:

    a) The gradual advent of drinking problems
    b) The slow disintegration of a marriage
    c) The deterioration of discipline in the home
    d) The slow drift away from God and church

Chapter 6 — **Foreign Objects in the Eye**

1. As a class project, write additional variations of Jesus' statement about planks and logs. Point out how the author did it (under the heading "Some Commonplace Specks and Planks"). Call on class members to share what they have written.

2. Encourage the members of the group to be very serious about doing no. 2 of the "Eye Exercises." A few "personal confessions" by the leader will encourage the rest to be honest with themselves and with others.

3. Discuss with the class the difference between making judgments and being judgmental. Try to include actual life situations.

4. Since this chapter, unlike the others, is based mainly on one passage of Scripture, you may want to do some additional research work. Ask your pastor for commentaries on Matthew, and see what the various scholars say about Matthew 7:3-5.

5. Today's "Eye Drops" are easy to memorize — a good opportunity to encourage faithful memorization.

Chapter 7 — **Black-sightedness**

1. Just for interest's sake, take a poll to see how many members of the group are aware of any color blindness in their own eyes.

2. Ask them to hold a hand over one eye and then the other, noting any difference in the color perception of the right and the left eyes. Some people can notice a difference. These same variations can exist between people, without anyone being aware of it.

3. Have three people enact a little pantomime. For instance, they can pretend they are sitting in church, singing. One of them scribbles a note and passes it to the others. One laughs and the other looks shocked.

Ask your group members to each write down what they believe was written on that note. Shuffle them and pass them around. Each person reads one of the interpretations. Is there evidence of black-sightedness? Note how easy it is to place a negative interpretation on things.

You may wish to develop additional original skits.

4. Discuss the implications of Titus 1:15. Can it be applied to all situations? What about viewing pornography, for example? What about classical nude statues? Nude photography? What causes one person to view mixed swimming as wicked and another person to see it as innocent? What about pictures of blood and violence?

Chapter 8 — Rose-sightedness

1. In this chapter we've shown how rosy words have been substituted for such concepts as drunkenness and lying. Have the class suggest rosy substitutes for *gossip, adultery, treason, racial discrimination, delinquency,* and other terms.

2. Ask each class member to write five additional items following the pattern of "You are overbearing; I am dynamic." Then ask each person to share his best one with the class.

3. Discuss with the class how a person can avoid the extremes of being black-sighted on one hand and rose-sighted on the other. What "helps" can a person turn to in order to check his opinions?

4. Discuss the question, Does a person's appearance

give reliable clues about his honesty?

5. This chapter may motivate you to invite a member of the local police department to speak to your group about common consumer frauds and confidence schemes. The senior citizens of your church should be particularly alerted to these dangers. The police department may also make available good literature on the subject.

6. If there is a schoolteacher in your church, ask him to share from his own experience the ingenious ways that parents use to avoid facing the truth about their children.

Chapter 9 — Green-sightedness

1. Give each person in the group a slip of paper and a pencil, and ask each to write down the one thing that most makes him see green. For instance, it may be a friend's new dress, or new furniture or money or attractive appearance. Assure them that the responses will be shared anonymously, since the slips will be collected and shuffled. Compile the results, announce them, and discuss them. The responses may surprise you.

2. Discuss whether it is easier to weep with those who weep or to rejoice with those who rejoice. Why? Is envy a possible factor?

3. Point out in what way Jacob was largely responsible for the jealousy that Joseph's brothers had for him. Using a chalkboard, make a list of suggestions that will help prevent or eliminate jealousy within families.

4. Have the group sit in a circle, the leader included. The leader will give a compliment to the person on the right. That person will give a compliment to the next person, and the compliments will continue until they have reached full circle. It's a good way to overcome envy.

Chapter 10 — Tunnel Vision

1. There may be some tension between this chapter on "Tunnel Vision" and the chapter on "Getting Used to the Dark."

I might, for example, believe that I am overcoming tunnel vision, while you might believe I am getting used to the dark.

How can we be sure that our new "broad-mindedness" isn't just a surrender of principles? Or, on the other hand, how can we be sure that the "courage of our convictions" isn't just narrow-mindedness?

2. Some discussion questions:

In what areas should Christians be able to "agree to disagree"?

Is it possible to respect another's opinions while staying true to one's own convictions?

What are some of the taboos you grew up with — taboos which you are happy not to impose upon your own children?

What do you think of ecumenical union worship services? With other denominations? With Roman Catholics? With Jews? What are the benefits and dangers?

3. Use the "Eye Exercises" as the basis for a group discussion. This could become rather lively.

Chapter 11 — Limited Vision

1. Bring samples to class of some of the items that reflect the intense craving of our time for advance knowledge of the future: horoscopes, "visions," "prophecies," interpretations of Bible prophecies, religious films on prophecy, "doom" booklets.

2. Find in the library some back issues of general circulation magazines that contain prophecies by well-known seers such as Jeane Dixon and Ruth Montgomery. Such articles are often found in the December or January issues; consult the *Reader's Guide to Periodical Literature* if you have trouble locating them. How many of the prophecies came true?

3. Discuss the various images of God that the class members have in their mind's eye. In what respects are

these concepts valuable? In what ways are they faulty?

4. Read the classic book by J. B. Phillips, *Your God Is Too Small* (published in paperback by Macmillan). It should be available in your church library or pastor's library.

5. Invite class members to relate the "meanings" they may have found in hardships, tragedies, and illnesses they have experienced. Invite them to relate hardships in which there was apparently no discernible meaning or purpose.

SCRIPTURE INDEX